EVER TRUE

A UNION PRIVATE AND HIS WIFE

CIVIL WAR LETTERS OF
PRIVATE CHARLES MCDOWELL
NEW YORK NINTH HEAVY ARTILLERY

Lisa Saunders

HERITAGE BOOKS
2011

HERITAGE BOOKS
AN IMPRINT OF HERITAGE BOOKS, INC.

Books, CDs, and more—Worldwide

For our listing of thousands of titles see our website at
www.HeritageBooks.com

Published 2011 by
HERITAGE BOOKS, INC.
Publishing Division
100 Railroad Ave. #104
Westminster, Maryland 21157

Copyright © 2004 Lisa Saunders

Other books by the author:

Play: *Ever True: One Couple's Journey through the Civil War*

The Military Coming of Age of William Henry Seward, Jr.
copyright © 2003 Peter Wisbey

The Man They Couldn't Kill
copyright © 2003 by Guy and William Aurand

Map (Ontario/New York) copyright © 2003 Marianne Greiner

All rights reserved. No part of this book may be reproduced or transmitted in any form or by any means, electronic or mechanical, including photocopying, recording or by any information storage and retrieval system without written permission from the author, except for the inclusion of brief quotations in a review.

International Standard Book Numbers
Paperbound: 978-0-7884-2526-4
Clothbound: 978-0-7884-8809-2

TABLE OF CONTENTS

Introduction		vii
Acknowledgements		xi
New York Ninth Heavy Artillery Timeline		xii
Who's Who		xiii
Part I	1862	
Chapter One:	Mustered in	1
Chapter Two:	Typhoid Fever	15
Chapter Three:	Lincoln Visits	20
Chapter Four:	The 138th becomes the New York Ninth Heavy Artillery	27
Part II	1863	
Chapter Five:	Defenses of Washington	31
Chapter Six:	Nancy Moves to Washington	39
Chapter Seven:	Fort Foote	50
Part III	1864	
Chapter Eight:	Nancy Contracts Typhoid Fever	55
Chapter Nine:	Rapidan Campaign (North Anna River/Cold Harbor/ Jerusalem Plank Road)	72
Chapter Ten:	Battle of Monocacy	93
Chapter Eleven:	Sheridan's Shenandoah Valley Campaign Battles of Opequon (or Winchester), Fisher's Hill and Cedar Creek	108
Chapter Twelve:	The Siege of Petersburg	122
Part IV	1865	
Chapter Thirteen:	Lee Surrenders, Lincoln Shot	129
Chapter Fourteen:	Mustered Out	148
Epilogue		159
Addendum	Secretary of State Seward *"The Man They Couldn't Kill"* by Guy and William Aurand	163

	"The Military Coming of Age of William Henry Seward, Jr." by Peter Wisbey	167
Recipes	"Boxes from Home"	171
Glossary	Definition of Terms	179
Bibliography		181
About the author		185
Index		186

ILLUSTRATIONS

Cover: Found in family papers. Charles McDowell marked as second from the left but cannot confirm. Photo of 7th New York Militia in 1861
Title Page: Private Charles McDowell (The New York Ninth Heavy Artillery) and Charles and Nancy McDowell

White House (Charles McDowell's Stationary)	vi
Nancy and Charles McDowell 1891 Sketches (Seth Cole)	vii

Who's Who:
    Bill Burt (The New York Ninth Heavy Artillery), Charles, Nancy, David, John, William, Hiram, and Hiram Jr. McDowell (unless otherwise noted, family photographs are courtesy of Richard and Mary Ann Avazian), William H. Seward Jr. (Collection of Seward House, Auburn, NY), Almira, Charles, John, and William Wager (Collection of the United States Military History Institute), Stephen Wager, Norman York (The New York Ninth Heavy Artillery)   xiii

In Heavy Marching Order (Hard Tack and Coffee)	5
Long Bridge (Charles McDowell's Stationary)	7
Spooning Together (Hard Tack and Coffee)	15
A Chimney on Fire (Hard Tack and Coffee)	19
Fort Foote (National Parks Service)	50
Rodman Cannons (National Archives)	53
Bell Plane Landing (Library of Congress)	75
Cooking Pancakes (Hard Tack and Coffee)	113
The Milk Ration (Hard Tack and Coffee)	136
Grand Review (Library of Congress)	153
Charles McDowell's Rifle: Courtesy of Lee and Lorraine McDowell	154
New York 9th Heavy Artillery (Library of Congress)	158
Charles and Nancy McDowell	159
Nancy McDowell in Later Years	160
McDowell Homestead	162
The William H. Seward Monument (The New York Ninth Heavy Artillery)	170
Lisa Saunders (Photograph by Margaret Forman)	185

MAPS

New York/Ontario (sketch by Marianne Saunders)	182
1864-65 VA Campaign (The Battles and Leaders of the Civil War)	183
The Forts of DC (The Battles and Leaders of the Civil War)	184

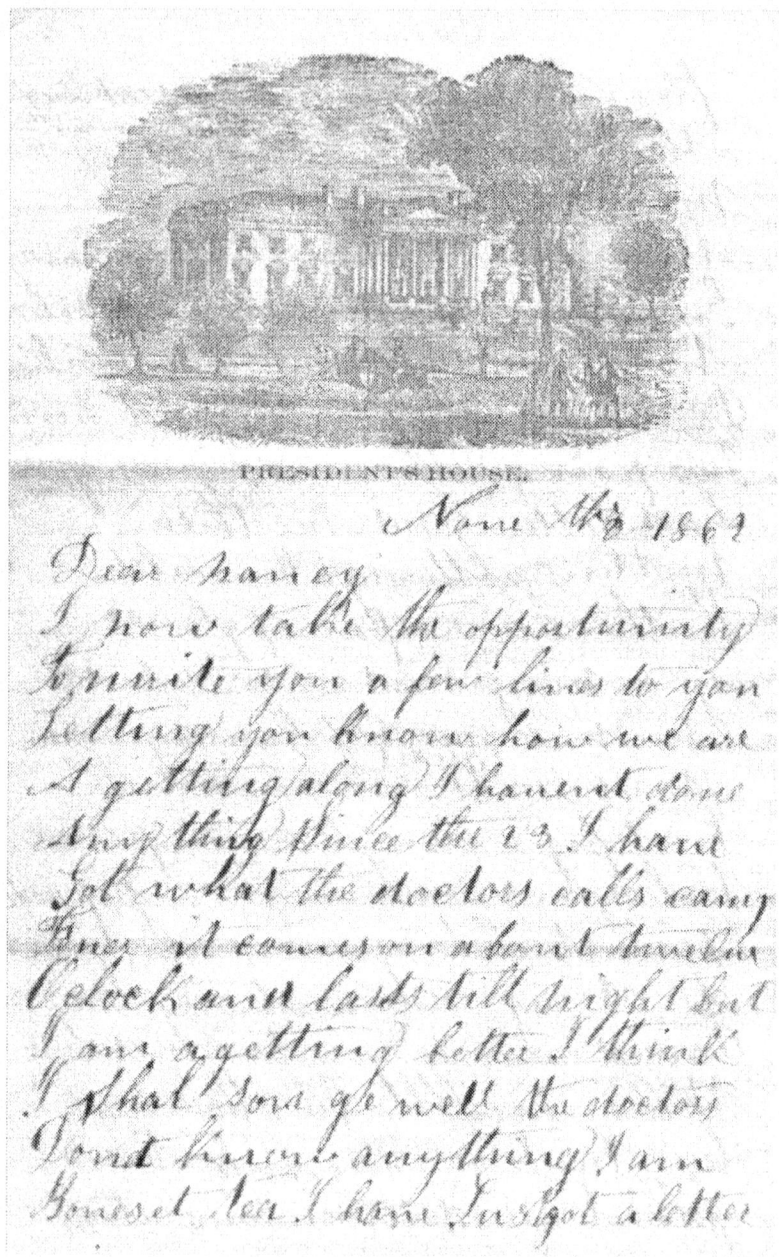

Charles's letter dated November 3, 1862 showing "President's House"

INTRODUCTION

Sketches of Charles and Nancy McDowell in 1891
Taken from Seth Cole

As a child I often visited the home Charles built after the Civil War in a little cross-roads called Alton, in western New York. My Aunt Nona and Uncle Gilbert lived there, along with my great-grandfather Bert McDowell. To me, Great-Grandpa Bert was just an old, wrinkly man who shuffled silently from room to room. The portraits of his parents, Nancy and Charles, in middle age, scared me as they guarded the living room. Their profiles appeared so grim that it was difficult to imagine that they had ever been young, or that they had even been real people.

The only thing I knew about them was that Charles had come from Canada and fought in the American Civil War, and that Nancy made and sold pies to soldiers when she joined Charles in Washington, DC. She even shook President Lincoln's hand. Nancy outlived her husband by many years and grew to be an irritable old woman. She made sure to visit the henhouse earlier than her live-in daughter-in-law Mary to grab all the eggs before Mary had a chance to collect them. Nancy made herself breakfast and kept the money from selling the rest. Nancy spent her last years rocking in her chair and looking out the living room window. One day she took a nap in that chair and never woke up. I used to stare at Nancy's rocker stored in the barn attic, terrified that her ghost would start it rocking again.

Almost one hundred and thirty years after the War, in 1992, when my husband Jim and I and our girls lived in Maryland, near Washington, DC, we came to visit my parents' home in Suffern, NY, for a family reunion. The subject of the Civil War came up.

"I heard that we had Charles's letters somewhere. Where are they?" I asked.

"They're in my attic," my mother said.

"They're in your attic! How come you never told me? I would love to see them."

"They're impossible to read. So faded, full of misspellings and poor grammar." My mother, a schoolteacher, can't tolerate bad grammar. Exasperated, she continued, "I only took them because your Aunt Nona was cleaning out the house and thought we really shouldn't throw them away, so I got stuck with them."

Within moments, I was crawling on my hands and knees through the tiny door that led to the cramped, stuffy section of their attic. I found the letters on the floor jammed in a small wooden box marked "Queen Bon Bons." They smelled old and dry, just like Nancy and Charles's home. As I carefully unfolded the stiff, yellowed letters I could scarcely contain my excitement. Some of the sheets bore line drawings of Civil War battles and the White House, while others were partially eaten away by mice.

Bringing them outside to the rest of the family, I tried to read one aloud. I had to admit, my mother was right. It was nearly impossible to understand the writing. My aunt Lorraine took one and seemed to have better luck. The very first one she read included the statement declaring that "Old Abe" had come around for a visit and he "looks about like any old farmer."

I couldn't believe that Charles had been stationed so near where I now lived! Perhaps he was even on some of those battlefields that Jim and I often passed on our way to somewhere else.

My mother said I could have the letters. I took them back home to Maryland and began what was to become an exciting ten-year adventure. First I arranged the letters from Charles by date and began to read. Once I grew accustomed to his old style handwriting and run on sentences (he never used periods and rarely used capitals), I felt myself leaving the present and entering his past. I traveled back 130 years and joined Charles in heart and mind. I felt his loneliness, his boredom, his fear. I laughed when he found a reason to laugh. I hurt over his deep longing for his wife and home and for the life and family he left behind in Canada.

Charles served under Secretary of State Seward's son, William Seward, Jr. in the New York Ninth Heavy Artillery. While stationed in the Circle Forts defending Washington DC, Secretary of State Seward (of "Seward's Alaskan Folly) regularly visited his son's regiment, and sometimes he brought along President Lincoln. As a result of these visits, the New York Ninth became better known as "Seward's Pets."

During his time in Washington, Charles survived "camp fever" and actually enjoyed life when Nancy came to live with him. According to her obituary, she too had the opportunity to speak with Lincoln and shake his hand.

But Charles's regiment did eventually suffer in the pain of the conflict between the North and South. He began serious soldiering when his regiment joined Grant's Army of the Potomac at the North Anna River and proceeded to the disaster at Cold Harbor. From then on, bullets and disease were his constant enemies. He no longer considered this adventure a thrilling diversion from farming--he just wanted it to end.

As the letters drew to an end, I was completely immersed in Nancy's anxious thoughts about Charles's welfare. She hoped there hadn't been a "ball made to kill" him. She longed for him to return to her-even if it was just for a short furlough. I now pondered the final years of her life spent rocking in her chair looking out the window. Perhaps she was awaiting her death so Charles could come for her once more.

Reading and typing the letters was exhilarating as I watched the story come to light after so many years of darkness. But it was also mentally exhausting. I could only tolerate deciphering them for about two hours a day before my head throbbed in protest at the faded, strange handwriting. Marjorie Perez, a historian from Wayne County, New York, graciously typed Nancy's letters which were even worse.

Although my husband Jim loved being a part of my background research, my oldest daughter, Jacqueline, tired of being dragged from one Civil War site to another. She recalls, "Instead of playing Barbies with my friends, I was forced to invite them along on battlefield tours to play soldiers. Once, when I cut my head on a plaque, and had to have my head bandaged by a park ranger, my mom cried, 'Great, now you look just like a wounded soldier. Lie down in that ditch so I can get a picture!'"

In compiling this manuscript I used several sources to provide background information for the letters. I consulted military records, history books, and particularly "The Ninth New York Heavy Artillery" by Alfred Seelye Roe, a fellow soldier of Charles. I spent many vacation hours visiting our upstate New York families and photocopying sections of Roe's 615-page volume, all the while wishing I possessed my own copy of this out-of-print book. Charles's picture is featured in a section about his company, and Roe personally thanked him in the preface for the contribution of his letters. I couldn't believe my luck when an Internet search found a copy in a used bookstore within a few miles of my home in Maryland. It cost me two hundred and seventy five dollars!

Many of the soldiers mentioned in Charles's letters or their widowed wives applied for disability pensions. I coerced my mother into spending her vacations in Maryland with me at the National Archives in

Washington loading spools of film onto a viewer so we could get the numbers that would lead us to our families' yellowed, forgotten files.

I thrilled at touching the actual letters from fellow soldiers and family members who wrote as witnesses stating that Charles was somewhat disabled from the effects of Typhoid Fever. I also opened the files of his friends and learned much about their illnesses and injuries as well as their lives afterward. I found that Private David McDowell, Charles's brother, was arrested for stealing chickens and a rowboat from Union farmers. Charles failed to mention this to Nancy, who happened to be the sister of David's lady friend.

Many others helped in the research. Historians added their insights into the letters, explaining the terms I was unable to decipher. Jim's cousin, Nancy Murinka, a volunteer at the Seward House in Auburn, N.Y., gave me a "behind-the-velvet-rope tour" of Seward's home where artifacts of the regiment are displayed. Now I understood why the young Mrs. Seward, just recovering from the birth of their first child, was able to hear the hushed whispers of her husband marching his regiment off to war. Her room faced the main road which was on their route to the train station.

I worked on the manuscript off and on for nearly ten years from 1992-2002. Finally, after taking three years off from the project to move back to New York and take a job as a recruiter working for my father in Suffern, I decided to tackle it again. In 2002, I spent my mornings before work at Starbucks or Village Wraps drinking coffee and editing my manuscript for possible publication.

In the interest of legibility, I corrected most spellings, added punctuation, and made paragraph separations. Most letters were originally one long run on sentence.

"Ever True" is a portion of the customary way people signed off on the letters. But it also holds another meaning: it speaks of the love that is ever true between Charles and Nancy and of their ever true sense of duty towards their country.

Most letters begin with "I now take pen in hand to write a few lines letting you know that I am well at present and I hope these few lines will find you the same." In most cases, for the sake of brevity, I deleted that opening line. Yet I hope that these many lines to follow will find you well and enjoying your journey through *EVER TRUE*.

ACKNOWLEDGMENTS

Many people, especially historians, friends, and family members, helped in the research and shaping of this book. Some dug up old census records, photocopied valuable information, scanned pictures, drew maps, typed letters, conducted archive searches, edited, advised, visited Civil War battlefields, baked Civil War foods, fitted me with a Civil War era dress, and just plain inspired me to persevere in this ten-year-long undertaking. A big, heartfelt thank-you to the following in alphabetic order:

Angie Amato of Village Wraps
Bill Aurand
Joan Asch
Dick and Mary Ann Avazian
Cynthia Bushnell
Larry and Patt Chester
Bill Clark
Laura Denke
Margaret Forman
Marianne Greiner
Mary Jo Holmes
Charles T. Jacobs
Amy Lipari
Cheri Major
Lee and Lorraine McDowell
The deceased McDowells that preserved and handed down the letters (Almira, Bert, Charles, David, Gilbert, Ida, Mary, Nancy, Nona, Russell)
Rose Miller
Nancy Murinka
Walton H. Owen II
Jerry Pooler
R.L.Murray
Jim, Jacqueline, and Elizabeth Saunders
Phyllis Saunders
The Seward House staff (Jennifer Haines, Paul McDonald and Peter Wisbey)
David and Janet Sisson
Terry Thiry
Wayne County Historical Society and their friends: (Debbie Ferrell, Kathy Hunt, Bruce and Sharon Lubitow, Kathy Marshall, Marjory Perez)
Corinne Will

THE NEW YORK NINTH HEAVY ARTILLERY TIMELINE

(Largely a Cayuga and Wayne County Regiment although men also from Albany, Genesee, Oswego, Onondaga, Ontario and Tompkins counties. Also Brooklyn)
Became part of the 3rd Division 2nd Brigade of the 6th Corps

Timeline: (The Civil War Archive Union Regimental Index New York: Regimental histories from A Compendium of the War of the Rebellion by Frederick H. Dyer, 1385)

Sept 1862-Aug 1863	Stationed near Washington DC
Aug 1863-May 1864	Built Fort Foote
May 18, 1864	Joined the Army of the Potomac
May through June	Rapidan Campaign
May 26	North Anna River
May 26-28	On line of the Pamunky River
May 28-31	Totopotomoy Creek
June 1-12	Cold Harbor
June 1-3	Bethesda Church
June 18-19	Before Petersburg
June 18-July 6	Siege of Petersburg
June 22-23	Jerusalem Plank Road, Weldon Railroad
July 6-8	Move to Baltimore
July 9	Battle of Monocacy
August 7 - November 28	Shenandoah Valley Campaign
August 21-22	Near Charlestown [Charles was in DC]
August 29	Charlestown [Charles was in DC]
September 19	Battle of Winchester
September 22	Fisher's Hill
October 19	Battle of Cedar Creek
Through December	Duty at Kernstown
December 3	Moved to Washington, DC, then to Petersburg
Dec 1864-April 1865	Siege of Petersburg
March 25, 1865	Fort Fisher
March 28-April 9	Appomattox Campaign
April 2	Assault and fall of Petersburg
April 5	Amelia Springs
April 6	Sailor's Creek
April 9	Appomattox Court House Surrender of Lee and his Army
April 17-27	Expedition to Danville
Till June	Duty at Danville and Richmond
June 8	Corps Review

WHO'S WHO

Margaret Brooks — Charles's sister, married and living in Canada

Bill Burt — Charles's comrade.

Eben Canfield — Charles's cousin, enlisted in Wisconsin. Missed the girls and sleigh rides.

Joe and Miss Cary — Charles's friend from Company C. It took a long time for the news of his death to be received.

Sam Lape — Charles's comrade. Promoted 2d Lieut

John Perkins — Charles's tent mate. Taken prisoner Monocacy; died Aug.18.'64, Danville Prison, VA.

Charles McDowell — "Charly." Born in Simcoe Canada.

Nancy Wager McDowell — "Nan," "Nat." Charles's wife.

David McDowell  Charles's younger brother and tent mate. Arrested for stealing chickens and a rowboat.

John McDowell  Charles's father.

Henrietta McDowell   Charles's step mother. Nicknamed Yetta

William McDowell  Charles's youngest brother

Hiram McDowell 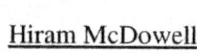 Charles's Uncle

Hiram McDowell  Charles's younger brother

Matthew McDowell   Charles's grandfather

James McDowell	Charles's cousin and a soldier.
Alfred Seelye Roe	Fellow soldier of Charles and author of The New York Ninth Heavy Artillery
William H. Seward	Secretary of State. See Addendum for assassination attempt.
William H. Seward, Jr.	In command of Charles's regiment. See Addendum for his career.
Sam Shannon	Charles's tent mate.
Almira Wager	"Mi," My." Nancy's Sister and David McDowell's lady friend.
Charles Wager	Nancy's father.
John Wager	Nancy's older brother who enlisted 10/15/61 in the 90th NY Artillery, Co. D. Died Key West 6/1/62 of typhoid fever.

William Wager   Nancy's cousin and tent mate of Charles.

Stephen Wager   Nancy's cousin. Enlisted with Nancy's older brother in 10/15/61 in the 90th N.Y. Artillery, Co. D. Transferred to 1st U.S. Art at Beaufort, S.C. Jan 63. Fought at Cold Harbor where he was wounded by a minnie ball in the right arm. Arm was amputated at the shoulder.

Norman York   Comrade and good friend of Charles and Nancy. Wife's name Lib. Taken prisoner at Monocacy, died Dec. 25, '64, Dansville Prison, VA. Buried there.

PART I

1862

Chapter One
Mustered in

Charles McDowell, a young farmer and recent immigrant to upstate NY from Ontario, Canada, received the following frantic letter from his Canadian father late in the summer of 1862:

Dear Son, [September] 1, 1862
    I feel a little uneasy about David [Charles's brother and neighbor] as he said in his letter that he was drafted and said he would do as I thought best. I wrote him a letter and told him to keep out of the war. I have not got no answer and I want you to do the same.
    Jonathan Hunt is in from the Michigan. Came here for fear of the war. He is married and left his wife in Michigan.
    Charles, I want you to see David and tell him to not join the army. If there is any danger he had better come home. Tell [him] I said so.
    Don't go in the war.
    Your affectionate parents till death.
    John McDowell

But this letter came too late to make any difference. Charles and his brother had already enlisted.
    A year earlier Charles's Canadian family had been happy...Granddad wrote:
    "*No war here, nothing but peace and plenty. Everything looks beautiful. I am sorry to hear of the war, but hope the North will come off victors. Give my respects to my brother and all his family...from your affectionate grandfather. Matthew McDowell.*"

Now, everything had changed. In July of 1862 Lincoln called for an additional 300,000 men to serve for three years. Battles such as Bull Run had shown the North that the war would not be easily won. That little

McDowell family in Canada now joined American families in their suffering. Charles and David joined weeks before receiving their father's pleas. It was probably difficult for them to resist when reading in their newspapers:

"To the Patriotic and Loyal Citizens of Wayne County
The country now calls upon you to rally to the support of its flag. Are you willing to let Jeff Davis, and his horde of rebels push upon your homes, pillage your houses and devastate your lands? Are you willing to be called traitors, poltroons, and cowards by the whole civilized world? Are you willing to see this great and glorious Constitution, which was won by the blood of your fore-fathers, trampled in the dust by a rebel foe? Are you willing to suffer the disgrace of being drafted when the foe is at your door? The Government believes not..." (The Clyde Times, Volume XII, Number 19, Wednesday, September 18th, 1861 Clyde, New York.)

Charles was twenty-five and his wife of one and a half years, Nancy Wager, was only seventeen when he enlisted in the Union Army in Lyons, New York on August 14, 1862. Nancy was still grieving for her brother, John Wager, who died a few months earlier while in the service of his country. Her parents had received the news from Nancy's cousin Stephen Wager of the 90th NY Artillery:

[Key West, Florida]
Dear Uncle and Aunt, *[May 3, 1862]*
I now sit down to write you the painful news that John is no more. He died in the afternoon of [May] the first. He had the typhoid fever. He was buried in the soldiers' burying ground the next day.
Dear Aunt Mary and Uncle Charles, you must not mourn yourselves sick for I believe John is in Heaven. He had been living a different life before he was taken sick and after he was sick he seemed contented and resigned. They sent for me about fifteen minutes before he died. I got their time enough to see him go and I believe he went in peace. He was out of his head for a good while before he died.
Your affectionate nephew Stephen

Now Nancy was facing the possibility that her new husband would share a similar fate. Upon Charles McDowell's enlistment in Lyons, Charles and Nancy traveled to Auburn, where the men of Wayne and Cayuga Counties were being organized into what would initially be designated the 138th Regiment New York Infantry. They were to serve under Secretary of State Seward's son, William H. Seward, Jr. Although that association did not protect Charles's regiment from marching to the front, it would bring him in close contact with not only the Secretary of State, but with President Lincoln as well.

William H. Seward, Jr. left his position in banking to become the Lieutenant Colonel of Charles's regiment.

The young Mrs. Janet W. Seward recalls the events leading up to her husband's departure for Washington with the regiment: "Of course we talked about my husband's going, but I was in hopes he would not have to do so; but one afternoon, while I was spending the day with my mother, who was not well, he came in with his hand behind him, sat down before me and unwrapped a parcel and gave to me a large photograph of himself. I knew instantly that he was going to leave me. I hope that I took it bravely, but I cannot exactly remember. After that, there were a great many preparations to make and the time went altogether too fast" (Roe, Alfred Seelye, The Ninth New York Heavy Artillery, Worcester, MA, 1899, 393)

In Auburn, while waiting to be sent to Washington, Charles McDowell lived among the other recruits in Camp Halleck, where he learned the basics of soldier discipline. The men slept in tents with three-tiered bunks; each covered with a thin pile of straw and a blanket. The ground where they lay and imagined the battles ahead is now covered with homes and located on what is presently known as Camp Street.

"Perhaps no more ludicrous incident is recalled of the story in Camp Halleck than that on parade, when Lieut. Colonel Seward's horse, like many of the soldiers, just from the farm, deliberately lay down, so frightened was he at the firing of the cannon. Even military dignity could not restrain the risibles of amused beholders" (Roe 17).

On the 8th of September, Charles, a member of Company D, was mustered into the service of the United States for three years. Within the next few days, he received his uniform.

On September 12, Charles was roused at 4:00 a.m. and began the greatest adventure of his life. But he began it quietly. They marched past Lieutenant Colonel Seward's house on their way to the train station, where Seward's young wife and newborn child lay sleeping. Janet Seward wrote: "On the 11th, our first daughter was born. On the 12th, very early in the morning, I was aroused by an unusual sound, and listening, found that it was the steady tramp of many feet passing the house. No other sound but a few words of command in a lowered voice that I knew so well. It was our regiment marching to take the train for Washington. It was really to me the most mournful sound that I ever heard. No drum, no fife, nothing but the quick, firm steps; and all the stillness was for my sake" (Roe 393-394).

Nancy was not at the train station to see Charles off. She returned to the home of her parents in Rose, N.Y.

To Nancy from Charles:

[New York City]   September the 13 - 1862
I thought I would take a few minutes to write to you letting you know how we are a getting along.

We started from Auburn Friday morning at eight o' clock and we was in New York Saturday morning at 6 o clock. We was met with great cheers all the way along. We are stationed right near Broadway and it's the liveliest place I ever see. They have the most ways for making money you ever see. They drawed us through the City with horses. Four horses to two cars and we had twenty-two passengers besides some freight cars.

We expect to get our guns before we leave here.

This is a beautiful place. We had two girls come and dance for us today. They both danced and played an accordion all at once. The nicest I ever saw.

I want you to write and let me know when you started for home. I looked for you all the next day. I didn't know whether you had gone or not but it was the lonesomest day I ever saw. I hope I will never feel so again.

Our guns has just come and I think we will start right off. Don't write till you hear from me again.

Your ever true and affectionate husband

To Nancy and Friends from Charles:

New York   [September] the 14, 1862
Dear Friends,

I now take the opportunity to write a few more lines to you letting you know that we are well at present and I hope you are enjoying the same comfort.

We have got our guns today and they are good ones. They have got on what they call sword bayonets. They have got a sheath on as same as any sword. You can use them in your hand or on the gun. [Roe called them "obsolete Belgian rifles."]

They say we are a-going to leave tomorrow morning at 6 o'clock but I wish we could stay here a month. It is such a splendid place. We had a nice meeting here today. Parson Brownlow spoke. The smartest speaker I think I ever heard.

Here is the place where you would see plenty of policemen. You will see one on every corner.

Your ever true and affectionate husband

When the regiment arrived in Washington on Wednesday, September the 17th, they little realized that that date was to become known as the bloodiest day of the entire Civil War. The Battle of Antietam was being fought only 50 miles away in Maryland.

Lee, heading north with his inferior number of troops, attacked McClellan. By nightfall Lee was defeated, but at great cost to both sides. 26,000 Americans were either killed, wounded, or missing.

That day and night, though fortunate to be far away from the battle, Charles's regiment faced their first exhausting march. Struggling under their heavy packs, they tramped through the dismal sights and smells of the open sewers of Washington towards Arlington, VA. At 9 p.m. they entered into Camp Chase.

"It was nearer midnight than sunset before the 138th had a chance to really rest...tired, saturated with perspiration, supperless, our boys lay, for the first time, with knapsacks as pillows, upon their overcoats and under their blankets.

"Thursday, the 18th dawned wet and drizzly, the direct result, every soldier knows, of the terrible day at Antietam, for rain always followed great battles..." (Roe 28)

In Heavy Marching Order. Courtesy of <u>Hard Tack and Coffee</u>

That afternoon they were ordered back to the District of Columbia to Fort Bunker Hill. Unable to make it back before night, they made camp, as well as their toilets, in the street.

Overcome by heat and fatigue, the regiment, with over 1,000 members, experienced their first death. "Porter V. Palmer of Company I, who had enlisted in Auburn, succumbed thus early to exactions and privations of a soldier's life. The physicians said the cause of his death was congestion of the brain. He was only nineteen years old, and his life of patriotism was ended almost before it began. The sad tidings circulated rapidly, and with hushed breath one comrade passed the statement to the next. Only two days before, at Antietam, more than 2000 brave boys in the Union army had fallen in fierce conflict, yet that loss did not have the effect upon these ranks that this one case from their own number had. Death was present, and his grim figure struck terror into hearts that otherwise feared not..." (Roe 30)

To Nancy from Charles:

Fort Bunker Hill   *September the 29 - 1862*
Dear Wife,

You wanted to know what ailed me. I had a very bad pain in my stomach and in my head but I feel first-rate at present.

I wrote to you this morning that we was a- going to leave. We got all packed up and ready to start and orders came for us to unpack and I tell you we wasn't sorry. The 137th took our place.

There is 9 forts right around here if you can see. They was firing the other day from twelve till 6 every half-hour for a captain that died. They fired at every fort. I was in one of them when they fired them. I tell you it made the ground tremble.

There was 15 hundred mules passed here the other day going to Washington.

I tell you the country looks bad here. Everything is a-going to rack. The weather seems altogether different here. The days is very warm and the night is cold. You can't get any cold water here. It's all warm and soft. We heft to be careful of what we eat here. We have had lots of sweet potatoes. They are 10 shillings a bushel and other potatoes is 1 dollar a bushel. Butter is 35 cents per pound. Milk is ten cents per quart. Cheese 20 cents.

There is five of us tents together. Me and S[am] Shannon, and David, J[ohn] Perkins, W[illiam] Wager.

I want you to call at South Sodus office. I expect a letter from Eb [his cousin, who according to Charles's family in an Aug 1861 letter, had "volunteered to fight the rebels in Wisconsin"].

Long Bridge. Sketch on Charles's stationary

We have crossed this bridge you see here when we went to Arlington Heights. I have been all around the Capitol. It's a splendid place. There is three hundred men to work at it now and we saw Washington Monument. It's a large thing.

They raise some tall corn here. The boys brought in a stalk that measured fourteen feet and nine inches. We went out today and brought in lots of tamarack boughs to lay on and we have got trees set before our door but washing dishes I don't like.

Yesterday I went and washed my shirt for the first time. We get plenty of soap here and we had aughta to keep clean and we live pretty well now.

We have new bread every day and we can cook for ourselves if we are a-mind to. There is four or five out of the company to cook and sometimes we cook for ourselves and sometimes we don't, just as we feel.

Your ever true and affectionate husband
So goodbye Nancy. I often think of you

"Our relations with the distinguished secretary of state, William H. Seward, were ever most friendly. As early as on our march to Camp Chase, this most courtly gentleman, in a carriage rode along our lines. On the 25th he came to Camp Bunker Hill, accompanied by an English officer, possibly Lord Lyons, then British minister in Washington, and was extremely cordial in his greetings, even alluding to us as his family and children. Naturally his interest in any regiment coming from his own home would be great, and reasonably it became greater in our case, since his son, his namesake, was second in command. As he often visited us, there need be little wonder that the 138th New York early acquired the nickname of "Seward's Pets." (Roe 34)

The government kept Washington heavily fortified in case the Confederates attacked the capital. Charles spent his days "drilling in infantry tactics, in light artillery as well as heavy, in fatigue duty and in strengthening the fortifications..."

The regiment was also required to appear for frequent inspection in full dress, leather stocks, white gloves and accoutrements shining like silver... they were derisively termed the `band box regiment'" (Clark, Lewis H. The County in the Civil War, New York: Clark, Hulett, Gaylord, 1883, 596-7)

To Nancy from Charles:

Fort Kearny　　　　　　　　　　　　　　　　　　　*Oct the 2-1862*
Dear Wife,
　　　We moved yesterday from Bunker Hill to Fort Kearny, about 8 miles distant and about five miles from Washington. It's a splendid place. We got here about two o'clock. We leave to here the place of [to replace] another regiment. We stopped near them and I went where they was and there was some of them had some boxes just sent to them filled with butter and cakes of all kinds and they give me a box about two feet- and- a- half square. It was filled with cakes and butter. It had about ten or twelve pounds of good Pennsylvania Butter in it and the rest was biscuit and sweet cake. I took it on my shoulders and took it down to my company and you had better believe they was glad to see it. I told them that it was sent to me from Wayne County and they all thought it was so and I ain't told them any different and I tell you it went good with us. Bill Burt said that [any] old box looked good that come from Wayne County.

　　　We are to work on the roads today. We haven't drilled any since we left. I don't know how long we will stay here but I hope we will stay here till the war is over. It's a splendid place.

　　　There is three hundred Negroes to work here on the fort.

　　　We have heard cannonading yesterday and today but we don't know yet where it is.

　　　There is great excitement in Washington about Lincoln going to Harpers Ferry. He went there yesterday. They say to see what they could do about settling this war.

McClellan was in Washington yesterday. You would laugh to see the mules here. Fifty and a hundred wagons in a string and from five to six mules hitched to a wagon.

And here is the place where you would see the timber slashed down. There [is] hundreds and hundreds of nice timber slashed down.

Your ever true and affectionate husband

To Charles from Nancy:

Dear Charly,   *October the 4 1862*

I was glad to hear that you had not left Washington.

You must not write on the outside of the paper again. I had to pay a sixpence [worth six pennies] before I could get it.

They have got the story around that Hank Converse's wife slept with Bill Burt a week or two at Auburn.

I want to know what your father thinks about your going to war.

From your true and affectionate wife Nancy McDowell

To Charles from Nancy's sister Almira Wager:

Dear Friend,   *October the 4 1862*

Nan [Nancy] thought that she was rich when she opened her letter to see the five-dollar bills in it. We have lots of peaches now. They lay all over the ground. I wish you was here to take tea with us tonight for we are a-going to have warm biscuits and butter and peaches and sugar and cream. I suppose it is only an aggravation to think of them but if you had stayed to home you might of had lots of them.

Yours truly,
Almira A Wager

To Charles from Nancy:

Dear Charly,   *October the 7 1862*

I was very glad to hear that they was a-going to settle this war but I am afraid that they won't. We are at work--all our peaches a- drying them. I wish that you was here to help eat them.

From your true and affectionate wife
You must not get discouraged.

To Charles and David from parents John and Henrietta:

Dear Children,   October 9, 1862
    We received you letter of the 25th of September. We was glad to hear from you and that you were well but was sorry to hear that you and David was in the army.
    The night we got your letter we did not sleep much. We all hope we shall see you both again face to face. People think they will have to give the South their liberty yet.
    Granddad is alive yet and sends his love to you both. Wishing your safe return.
    I am sorry you enlisted but it [is] too late. I will remember you in my prayers.
    I got a letter from David saying he would send me some money if he could without hurting himself. I would be thankful, as it is hard times with me at present.
    I cannot refrain from tears. I pray God that you both be spared to come home again. I want you very [much] to avoid all the danger possible. I want you to write as often as you can.
    There is not a night we lie down but we think of you and David. I shall be glad when the war is over.
    I must bring my letter to a close, so goodbye Charles, goodbye David. May the all-wise hand protect you both.
    Remain your affectionate parents till death.
    John and Henrietta McDowell
    I want you to put this away and keep it.

To Nancy from Charles:

Fort Kearny   Oct the 10-1862
Dear Wife,
    I have just found a pen. Sometimes we have a dozen pens and sometimes we ain't one. But something seems curious that I don't get a letter from you. I begin to think that you have forgotten me aready. I can't think though Nancy but what you would write when you can because you know what you said before we parted

and I know your word to be good. Most all the boys has got a good many letters and they say you have forgotten me but you know I don't believe that.

I remain your ever true and affectionate husband

To Charles from Nancy:

Dear Charles,   *Tuesday October the 14 1862*
I went clear to Alton [8 miles] last night to get a letter but could not get any. If I don't get one tomorrow night I don't know what I shall do. I have written two letters since I have had any. The boys writes home that they don't have enough to eat and that they sleeps cold. I think that it must be very hard to suffer so.

We have got done a- drying peaches. Ma give me all that I dried. I have got about twenty pounds. We are to work on the apples now.

Pa has got his potatoes all dug. He has got sixty bushel. He has his corn all cut.

All of the folk gits letter but I do not get any. Samuel Lape's wife gits letters from Sam about every mail.

Eliza Thompson has got well now. The girls is a- having their hairs cut all off from their heads [it was believed that cutting hair helped in the healing process—like the way pruning a tree keeps it healthier].

Most of the folks thinks that the war will end before long. I hope that it will for it seems that you have been gone a long time. I think that I have a lonesome time but when I think of you how you haft to suffer out there I think that I had not ought to grumble.
From Nancy McDowell

To Charles from Nancy:

Dear Charly,   *Oct the 15 1862*
It is very dry here. The well is all dry and cistern is dry.
They will not take stamps around here no. They have shinplasters [see glossary] now. I have sold about four dollars worth of meat of ours.

You said that you thought that I had forgot you but I never will forget you the longest that I live. I have written a great many times and I am not to blame if you do not get them.

Pa is a-picking up cider apples. He is a-going to make cider now. Almira is writing to David.

To Nancy from Charles:

Camp Nelly Seward [named after Seward Jr.'s newborn daughter]
Dear Wife,   Oct the 17-1862
I now take another opportunity to write a few more lines but if it don't do any more good than the rest that I wrote it won't do much now then.

I haven't had one letter since I have been here. I have wrote as much ten letters and I tell you it seems rather discouraging but if I thought that you had got my letters and had not written to me I wouldn't never put my hand to a pen to write to you again but I can't hardly think but what you would write but it seems curious we have been here about three weeks and I ain't had a letter.

We are to work on the fort now. We are turned into the artillery. We are a- going to have a new suit of cloths. We had a great time here the other night. We heard the news that rebel Cavalry had crossed the Potomac and we all had 40 rounds apiece. Our company all was in the fort. We kept out guns in our hands all night but they say they went back.

They say Garibaldi [of Italy] is a-coming with his army but it's only a report. [Lincoln offered Garibaldi a command in the Union Army but he declined].

We don't see a white woman here from one weeks end to another but there [is] lots of n___er wenches and the rest is all soldiers. If you see all the soldiers here you would think Uncle Sam couldn't stand it a month.

Well I don't know that there [is] any use of writing any more.

From your ever true and affectionate husband

During this time that the New York Ninth spent building forts and roads, the men often sang to the tune of Dixie:
'I wish I was in old Wayne County

My three years up, and I had my bounty
Look away, look away,' etc." (Roe 39).

To Nancy from Charles:

Fort Mansfield   *Oct the 19-1862*
Dear Nancy,

I received three of your letters last night and you may believe I was very glad to receive them. We have moved again. We left yesterday and marched about three miles near Fort Mansfield. There is six forts within a mile. We are about a mile-and- a- half from Chain Bridge on the Potomac. You can see the river from here.

You wanted me to write something about the country. Well I will tell you it's a dreary looking country. No fences, no nothing but desolation. The fences is all burnt up and the woods that was standing is all cut up with roads and forts and if they have cornfields the soldiers would just as leave run through it as not. When we marched here I was taken as one of the guard and I was stationed next to a turnip patch and in less than half an hour it was covered with our soldiers and that's the way with them. They run over everything and tear up everything they come to. Their barns is poor and their houses is poor and the folks that lives in them is poor and they don't seem to be over half- witted. They seem to be lazy and dull but they say three or four miles from here it is quite a country. We are within six miles of Washington.

Our boys is all [laying] around today. Some is writing and some is sleeping and some is running around. You wanted to know how we fared about our bed and board. Well the most of them sleeps warm enough. Some I hear complain but we sleep warm enough in our tent. We use cedar boughs to lay in the bottom of our tent. And what we get to eat is pork and it is good too. We have beef once or twice a week and we have fresh bread every day and all we want and coffee twice a day and sometimes tea. Sometimes we have potatoes two or three times a week and sometimes less. And sometimes we have rice and sometimes we don't. We don't have much regularity but if we don't fare any worse we will get along but we don't live like we did when we was to home. We can't expect it.

But I tell you this war is an awful thing. I can't begin to tell you anything about it but I can tell you things that you wouldn't never thought of, or me either, but I will wait till I come home.

I suppose you will think I sent you a pretty sorry letter but you must excuse me for I felt very lonesome. I didn't know what to do to get a letter.

To Nancy from Charles:

Camp Morris   Oct the 22-1862
Dear Nancy,

We are having good times here now. Some of the boys begins to think they will soon have their poll tax soon worked out but I had rather work on the roads than to go and fight.

We went out on a little scout the other day. We went out to a house and we called for a Johnnycake[also called hoecakes - a Confederate pancake made from corn meal] and some milk but the women said that the boys had [emptied] the cows last night. The boys thought that was funny but she went to work and made us a big cake and baked in one of the old fashioned spiders [iron pan with feet on it] before an old-fashioned fireplace. We[ll] it soon cooked and when it was done she wrapped it in a cloth and Bill Wager took it under his arm and we followed him. Just as we turned round the corner of the house there we saw some pigs tied up with ropes and each one had a bell on it.

Well we went to our tent and we got some molasses and we had a good dinner. It is awful cold nights here now but we haven't had any frosts yet but awful heavy dews.

The opinion of the people is that the war won't last long. I hope it may be true but they can't tell but they say the rebels is in a bad condition. Now the boys is pretty well run ashore for money. The pistols that they bought [in] Auburn and give fifteen dollars for they are selling them for five and a half and it's just so with all the things that they bought. They think more of ten cents than they did of ten dollars when they first came here. If they could have bought whiskey they would have been out of money in two days after they got here, the most of them, but you can't get that for love or money.

I don't know how it's a- going to go this winter with five in a bed. They kick round a good deal. We set our dishes to our feet

the other night and in the morning the[y] was all kicked out in the street. That's the way they do here.
    I remain your ever true and affectionate husband

Spooning Together. Courtesy of Hard Tack and Coffee

Chapter Two
Typhoid Fever

    The following day (Oct 23rd) Charles came down with Typhoid Fever and was very ill for a long time. It wasn't until the end of December that he was strong enough to stand guard. He later applied for disability, claiming the disease left him with a weak heart and pain in the side.

To Nancy from Charles's family:

Dear Daughter,   *October 25, 1862*
    I feel to sympathize with you about Charles going to the war. Sorry am I that either one of them went. I have written to Washington to the British minister to get David out but failed. They will have to run their chance. But it is a slim chance for them.
    I have had letters from both of them. I hope you will be reconciled to your lot. It gives us a great deal of trouble because they went in the war but it is done and there [is] no help for it now.

I hope we shall meet again face to face but if we never on the earth shores of time I hope we shall meet where parting will be no more.
Remain your true parents till death.

To Charles from Nancy:

Dear Husband,   *October the 26 1862*
I was at meeting to York Settlement. There was not many there for it stormed so. This morning, when I got up, the ground was all covered with snow and it keeps on snowing yet. If it keeps on so much longer, we will [be] sleighing.

I want to know if you don't want some mittens for [I] should think that your hands would be cold when you stand on guard

To Charles from Nancy:

Dear Husband,   *Tuesday evening October the 28 1862*
Almira went over to Mr. Winchet's yesterday and I had to sleep alone last night. I had so much room that kicked around like everything. I wish that you had been here to have help filled up the bed.

I talk of sending you some dried peaches and I want to know if you could stew them if I sent them. I was to Samuel Lape's the other day and read his letter and he said that the enemy had fired at the regiment and one of the balls past about two feet over his head. He said when he heard them fire that he did not know whether he should see home again or not.

Leonard Camp's wife has not got no letter yet. She has tried to runaway from the asylum but they caught her.

We have just got our stove set up today and it looks like old times. It makes me think of you every time I look at it.

I remain you true and affectionate wife
my pen is ___ and
my ink is pail and
my love for you will never fail

To Charles from Nancy:

Dear Husband,   *November the 2 1862*
    We got a letter from Stephen Wager last Friday night. He was well and he has had the Yellow Fever but he made out to live through it.
    George Angle is dead. He had the fever and he had got so that he was around the house and then they baked a lot of Johnnycake and he eat so many that it killed him.
    I am very lonesome here today. I wish that you was here today. I don't think that I would be lonesome then. The folks think that there will be another call for more men. I do not see where they will come from.
    I think that your father is a little grouty towards me because you went to war or else I think that he would have written to me. You wrote about you're a-coming home in two or three weeks to eat some dried peaches. Oh how I wish that you could come home. I tell you that we would have a happy time. If you want me to send you something to eat, write and tell me what you want and I will sent it to you. The way that you wrote about you and Bill Wager [Nancy's cousin] a-going after the Johnnycake, I don't think that you have enough to eat.
    I remain your true and affectionate wife.
    Oh you don't know how much I want to see you.

To Nancy from Charles:

Dear Nancy,   *Nov the 3-1862*
    I haven't done anything since the 23rd. I have got what they doctors calls camp fever. It comes on about twelve o' clock and lasts till night but I am getting better. I think I shall soon get well. The doctors don't know anything. I am [drinking] boneset tea [made from an herb used to treat fevers and malaria].
    You may send some peaches and some dried apples[and] a blanket. David wants you to send him two pair of socks and I guess you had better send me them mittens although I would rather have a pair of gloves. You may send us some butter. Send me a quart of brandy and send us each a tick just big enough for one person to lay on. Send us some peppermint oil. You want [to] do it up in a strong

box. David wants you to send his woolen muffler. The other boys has just written to their folks to send them some stuff and we thought if you kindly would fix it up together I think it would come cheaper. Send me a little money for I am out and we got to buy a stove. Send some bitter root. If it wouldn't be very convenient, you needn't send the blanket now.

   Your ever true and affectionate husband

   David wants you to send him a good pair of gloves. You had better send the box by express. We don't care how cheap the ticking is as long as it will hold straw.

November 5, 1862: President Lincoln replaces General McClellan with Major General Burnside as head of the Army of the Potomac. Although McClellan is very popular with his men, Lincoln is frustrated by McClellan's reluctance to use his troops to fight against Lee.

To Nancy from Charles:

Camp Morris   *Nov the 8-1862*
Dear Nancy,

   I am a- getting quite well. I think I have got my fever almost broke up. I am so that I walk out to the neighbors. I think I will be all right in a few days.

   We had quite a time last night. We got a stove the other day and last night we had a fire in it and we left wood against it and we laid down and went to sleep and we hadn't been asleep long when some of us waked up and found the wood by the stove all in a blaze and such a-scrabbling you never saw. They soon had the stove in the street. It didn't burn our canvass much but burnt Bill's hands all to a blister.

   We had two or three inches of snow here yesterday but it about all off today. If you think that any other kind of liquor would be better than brandy get it. I wouldn't go to the druggist to get it. It costs so much.

To Charles from Nancy:

Dear Charly,   November the 9 1862
  Pa is a- going to put the bitter root in the brandy. They say that he cannot send it [the brandy] if he does not. I am a-going to send you a bottle of camphor to take so that you won't take so much peppermint. It ain't very good to take so much peppermint. It give some the piles [hemorrhoids]. We have got the box all packed and Pa is a-going to send it tomorrow. Ma sent that big roll of butter.
  I am a-going to send you five dollars. I don't think that will be too much.
  I remain your true and affectionate wife

To Nancy from Charles:

Dear Nancy,   Nov the 16-1862
  Our box came last night all safe and sound and was glad to see it but that brandy I don't know hardly how to take it. If it wasn't mixed I would know how to manage it. I should thought they would have let you had it without being mixed.
  We are here to work on the roads yet. Two of our companies has gone about a mile from here. They have gave us a fort. You heard that we only got ten dollars a month and heft to stay our three years but that ain't so. We get our thirteen dollars a month just the same and we will be discharged just as quick for there is regulars enough to take our place. We have stewed some of them dried apples and they go first-rate. But nothing taste so good to me as them pickled peaches. They taste about right. I am most sorry that you sent my kid gloves but I guess I can manage them. It is nice weather here now but I don't know how long it will last. Oh I have just thought of that pump and well that Pa Wager was a-going to send down to us. If we had a Wayne County well here the whole regiment would be to it in less than five minutes.
  The boys has built stone chimneys and put a barrel on top and the other night one catched a fire and burnt up the tent and about thirty dollars worth of stuff.

Chimney on Fire. Courtesy of Hard Tack and Coffee

You didn't send me any too much money because I had to borrow some to buy me some milk and few other things to eat.

There has a great many bets been made in the regiment about the war. A good many has bet it would be settled by spring, but we can't tell, but one thing I am certain sure of, it can't last long.

I think we will have nice time when we get in a fort. The boys is just going on dress parade. They all go on dress parade Sundays but no other day.

The way they cook here they dig a hole right in the ground and have crotches [?] and pails and they hang their kettles right on and throw the wood right under the kettle. That's the way they do it.

To Miss Nancy McDowell from C McDowell

Chapter Three
Lincoln Visits

"Sunday, November 2d, at dress-parade, Secretary Seward and President Lincoln are present. Already hints are made that the 138th is a pet regiment. One of the boys thus describes the visit:' Just as the regiment, in fine condition, was drawn up in line, an open barouche [a four-wheeled carriage] was discovered in front on the right, in which were seated two distinguished looking men. Every eye observed them, though the command was, 'Front.' Shortly after Colonel Welling had taken his place, one of these men left the carriage and moved slowly to a position a little back of the colonel. By this time every man knew he was in the presence of Abraham Lincoln. The secretary remained in the vehicle. How proud we all felt! The sublime and the ridiculous are often mingled, and this event was an illustration. In passing the president, one of the officers, noted more for his stature than for his gracefulness, after sundry reproofs to his men for not keeping in step, apparently formed the resolution to measure heights with Mr. Lincoln as he passed. So at the proper moment he straightened up to all the height that God had given him, and evidently wished his men to make note. They did, for they heard the president say, distinctly, 'Lieutenant, I am taller than you.' The tall officer's collapse was never forgotten. Later many favored ones grasped the president's hand." (Roe 41)

To Nancy from Charles:

Dear Nancy,   *Nov the 19-1862*
I am gaining pretty fast. I think I shall soon be able to do duty.

We are having some mud here now. We have got one little log house up but we don't know how long we will stay here. They talked of moving in a day or two but we are a- going to move only a little ways.

We have [Secretary of State] Seward down here about every other day and sometimes he fetches Old Abe with him and looks about like any old farmer.

I spose you have plenty of snow out there. We ain't none here only once two or three inches. We have hung our dried fruit up around. I tell you it looks a good deal like house keeping. We have got enough to last us quite a spell.

I will send you this little book when we took supper to Baltimore. Our plates was turned upside down and one of these little books laid on the bottom of every one of them and I have kept mine till now and I thought I would send it to you.

Mary Ann Butt's man has laid in the hospital at Washington a long time. She wanted me to go and see him. I think I shall when I get better. All the rest of the boys in our tent is well.

I remain your ever true and affectionate husband
Goodbye Nancy. I often think of you.

To Charles from sister Margaret Brooks:

Norwich [Canada]
Dear Brother Charles,   November 20, 1862
    I see Charles by your likeness that you have failed since I saw you. It is either trouble or over fatigue but Charles you must have had a hard heart to went and leave your young and affectionate wife. I can sympathize with poor Nancy although I never had the trial and hope I never shall. I am going to write a letter to Nancy although we are strangers. I am sorry to think we are so far separated but I hope there is better times a- coming.
    Granddad is here now. He sends his love to you both. He is quite smart for him. You said I had forgotten you but I have not nor never shall as long as life lasts.
    I suppose Charles you have not forgotten the good old times we have had together. It would take up too much room and you know as well as I do, so goodbye dear brother till I receive an answer. Direct your letter to Princeton P. ...C. W.
    From your affectionate sister
    Margaret ...Brooks

To Charles from his cousin James McDowell:

[Canada]   November 20, 1862
Dear Cousin,
    We are all well and hope you are the same but Charly you have got a great war of a most to fear I am afraid. I am afraid I never shall see you but I hope I shall.
    Oh Charly I should think you would often think of the good times you have had here. Oh I wished you had a- stayed here.
    Say Charly, if you can slip out sly you had better. They wouldn't know but you had got discharged.
    Uncle Monroe was here a spell ago. He was astonished when I told him you was in the war. I spose you think it was most time I was married. Well I think I shall this winter if nothing happens. But Charly, if you can't come now you must come as soon as the war is over.

How do you get along without your wife seeing you once and awhile, didn't you get a furlough? But they think here the war won't last long. Hope it won't.
I remain your ever true and affectionate cousin,
James McDowell

To Charles from Nancy:

Dear Charly,   November the 20, 1862
The regiment left Auburn last night. There was about 12 of the men refused to go. But after a while, they all consented to go, but two of them, and they swore that they would not go and they took their knives out and was a-going to kill their Capt[ain] and he shot them dead on the spot.
[The] brandy you said that you did not know how to take it. You must take about a spoonful every morning. If it works on you, you need not take quite as much. The brandy cost twelve shillings. We heard that the officers examined it and if they found liqueur in it they would keep it, box and all, so Pa thought that he would put some root in it.
I sent that camphor. It is good to break up the chill. You must take it just before it comes on. I am a-going to send you some wild turnip to take for your fever. You can take it in water or anything you like.
You must be saving of your butter. You must not let John and Sam eat it up from you. You wanted to know how the box cost. It cost ten shillings [a shilling is worth 12 pence. A pence is the plural for pennies] a piece. I paid for the peppermint. It cost 18 pence. The camphor 20 cents. You wrote for me to send you some preserves. I can't send you any now. You must stew your peaches. Stew them slow and they will be about as...
Ma got me a dress, cost four dollars, for helping dry apples. We got a letter from Stephen Wager [her cousin, a Union soldier] and he was well.
You must write often and keep up good courage.
From your true and affectionate wife

To Nancy from Charles:

Nov the 28-1862

Nat [Nancy] I thought I would write a few more lines before I went to bed.

They say the news is now that Burnside sent a dispatch this afternoon to Lincoln and wanted to know if he should burn Richmond. I think he is a- going to do something.

There is a considerable many of the boys sick but I never felt better than I do tonight but I ain't very strong. These doctors don't [know] nothing. One of them is under arrest. If I had took all the medicine that they gave me I think I would have been dead now. I had a double handful of [quinine] powders but all I took was three or four. I got boneset and one thing or other. I sent to town and got half a pint of whisky and some pernnen [?] bark and some cream tarter and one or two more things and it helped me right along. I tell you I believe in doctoring myself.

We can sleep warm and nice as can be. Our little house is most full of blankets.

I could write you a good deal about some of the boys, but then it's against our rules. Well not my rules, but theirs, because I ain't a-going to do anything that I am ashamed to have them write about, but if I was in the place where some of them is, I should think I would be then. I will tell you when I come home.

The officers uses me quite well. They tell me that I mustn't go out till I get all right. I must now go to roll call.

From your ever and affectionate husband.

Goodbye Nat. How I would like to see you but keep good courage.

Bill Wager is very sick. He was taken last Saturday. He has got the fever but I hope he will soon get better.

To Charles from Nancy:

Dear Charly,   November the 30, 1862

I think that Alford Courtright done well when he got married to that woman. She comes to Old Courtright the other day and she was so drunk that she come in she fell down behind the stove and she laid there a long time.

Sary Tindall is getting smart. What made her sick she took

a box of female pills. Paw has just killed his hogs and we made some sausage. If you could cook some I would send you some.

We have meetings here every week but I don't like to go so I hafto stay home alone.

Bill Burt just showed himself. He went just to cheat folks. He put his property all out of his hands. He has cheated Bradley Camp out of eighty dollars and that haint half what he has cheated.

From your ever true and affectionate wife.

I have just heard that you have been turned into the heavy artillery. I want you to write and tell me all about it.

To Charles and David from Nancy's father Charles Wager:

Dear Friends,   *December the 8 1862*

I often think of you. Today we have killed the fat cow and have hung it up on the same place that we had the other one and I want David to come home and help cut it up and I want Charly and Dave to come home and help eat it.

You wrote about Lincoln goin to Harpers Ferry to settle the war. Since Lincoln's last proclamation come out I think that he had talk with the freed men. I think that he knows about how they feel. I think that the [war] will be settled between this and April but seeing you are there you must keep up good courage. It may come around all right.

I remain your ever true and affectionate friend.

To Nancy from Charles:

Dear Nancy,   *Dec the 14-1862*

You never see any one gain so fast as I have. I was to Washington last Tuesday and I weighed a 154 1/2 aready. I don't know what I will weigh if I keep on as I have done. I am afraid I am a- gaining most too fast.

I went through the patent office and through the Capital. I tell you it is a great sight. There is hundreds of people there every day. There is pictures there that cost over two thousand dollars a piece but there is some curious things in the patent office. I saw Washington whole suit sword and you can see everything else.

I saw a-going there a lot of soldiers going to bury a general. There was a thousand [soldiers] on foot with their guns and behind them was a thousand cavalry and behind them was ten cannon. Each drawed by ten horses and behind them was the corpse and behind them was as much as fifty carriages. It was quite a sight.

It is like summer here now. There are drafting here in Maryland. They drafted seven hund[red] last week. They have got to go Thursday. They have took Fredericksburg.

Sam Lape is most well. He ain't thought much of in the company. They ain't got our tents done yet.

The next letter I send you, I don't want you to show it to any body.

We are fixing for Christmas. We are going to have mule soup but that's nothing new. The boys' ears begins to stick up [awfully]. I don't know whether I shall have roast goose or not. I want you to put these letters away. Write as soon as you can.

Charles McDowell

To Charles from Nancy:

Dear Husband,   Dec the 14 1862

I received your kind letter and was glad to hear that you was well but was very sorry to hear that Bill Wager was sick.

It is quite warm now. The snow is all gone again.

We heard that six of the picket guard froze to death. Poor boy[s]. I think it is very hard to suffer so when they have enough and some to spare at home.

Uncle David's folks is quite worried about Bill [Wager]. I want you to write about him. I want to know if he is better or not for I think it is very hard to be sick so far from home.

Thompson folks got a letter from Samuel. He wrote that he was on the road to Richmond. He wrote that they expected a hard battle before long.

The Lyons papers is not good for nothing so I thought that I would not sent it but when it is got some thing worth sending I will sent it. I haven't heard from Eb [Canfield] yet. Poor fellow. I am afraid that he is dead.

From your ever true and affectionate wife

There is a band of pilgrims
That walk the narrow road
I do believe they will conquer
And ware the Snow-white robe
When we lay down the cross then
We will take up the crown
And we will follow our Jesus all the way long

To Charles Wager (Nancy's father) and friends from Charles:

Dear Friends,   *Dec the 14-1862*
    I should like to get a holt of a piece of that beef you killed. I would hang on and growl but then what is the use of talking beef. Nothing to what we have. We have the nicest mule beef you ever see. The boys ears sticks up so now you can't hardly see their heads and they are getting so mulish you can't hardly do anything with them.
    Old Abe and Seward was here tonight and said that yesterday that there was five thousand of our men killed and wounded yesterday just the other side of Fredericksburg. He says they are fighting today awful. He said they drove them three miles yesterday. They stand our folks a good piece but I hope we will whip them. If they whip us there it will about use us up but if we whip them I think the hard fighting will be over with.
    I tell you there is stirring times here now. They was carrying off the dead and wounded all last night. I tell you the times will be awful for a week to come. Some of the officers is afraid if they beat us we will be sent on but we will know tomorrow.
    I should like to be there to spend Christmas and New Years but I am afraid I shant. Little did I think last Christmas that I would be a way off here now venturing my life for the country. [The previous Christmas Eve he was celebrating his first wedding anniversary with Nancy].
    I must go to roll call now.
    I remain your ever true and affectionate friend

Chapter Four
The 138th becomes the New York Ninth Heavy Artillery

To Nancy from Charles:

Dearest Nancy,   *Dec the 21-1862*
    You said you heard that there was six men froze to death. That ain't so but is pretty cold nights but it quite warm day times. One of our men the other day got a bullet shot through his hand. Him and another fellow was a-fooling and one of their guns went off. They think he will heft to have his hand taken off. They have taken two of his fingers out now.
    Bill Wager is most well. It begins to look some like home because the women is getting pretty plenty. There was thirteen come in last Saturday. Soldiers women. Mary Ann Butts' man is got his discharge. They don't expect him to live.
    It is drawing pretty nigh Christmas. I don't know what we shall have but I guess not much. I am sorry it is so I can't be with you this Christmas but I am afraid I can't but Nancy you must try and enjoy yourself as well as you can but I hope by another Christmas we shall enjoy ourselves together. And if another war breaks out I think I will take your advice although our work ain't nothing.
    Our colonel and his wife has gone home. Our new barracks is most done. I am much oblige to you for that paper and envelope but I would have been more oblige for a stamp [stamps were three cents]. Maybe you think I don't write often enough but I'll tell you Nat postage stamps is pretty scarce but never mind. I will try and get along and write oftener.
    We have got to go on dress parade now. We are done working on the roads. The old man Seward has resigned his office. [Lincoln did not accept his resignation].
    We had a good dinner today. We had fresh beef and potatoes and beef soup and bread and tea or coffee. Just which you liked best.
    There was another had two of his four fingers shot off today by fooling.

It's a bad place to write here. There is so much talking and moving against one another. We have got lots of dishes. We went out when some of the regiments left here and we got all we could carry. They heft to leave an awful sight of stuff.

I was on guard the other night and I liked to blow away. Our orders was read to [us] last night that we was in the artillery. We will soon have a new suit.

They say here that we lost between twenty and thirty thousand men at that battle of Fredericksburg, killed and wounded. There was three thousand wounded come into Washington in forty-eight hours. What Burnside is a-going to do now I can't tell.

I remain your ever true and affectionate husband.

So goodbye Nancy

To Charles from cousin Eben Canfield (enlisted in Wisconsin):

New convalescent Camp near Fort Barnard by the way of Washington D.C.   *December 22, 1862*
Dear Cousin Charly,

My health is getting quite good. They have tried to kill the old fellow but can't commit this time. I will not attempt to tell you all the changes I have made since I saw you as it would take more than this sheet to do it but let it suffice that I am now a few miles west of Washington City on the sacred soil of Old Virginia (made so by the dead bodies of our men) living in a tent with 4 others of my Company who like myself have been back sick. They are all good fellows & we have the best tent in the camp (we have been in the service long enough to look out for number one). By putting 2 together we have a cook room & bedroom. Our bed is a large one as we all sleep together & we have nothing else to do but sleep & eat & hunt rabbits when we feel like it which is good sport so we make out to pass the time quite easy but I cannot say pleasantly for there is that lack of society that makes a young mans life pleasant. But as my very indulgent Uncle [Sam] has got a tight hold of me, I have got to make the best of it & look ahead for better times in the <u>future</u>.

I will give you a description of our Christmas dinner. It <u>was a splendid affair</u>. We got word a few days before the eventful time that the Convalescent Camp was to have a great dinner of all the good things of life. Well Christmas came, & shortly after the Ladies provisions, but they had not rightly estimated the number of our Camp & after calling out all the Conv[alescents], found that they had only enough for the New York & Penn - troops. The <u>Western</u> troops as <u>usual</u> were told to go to their quarters. I started for my tent at that command. I had received a clay pipe & went back puffing like a steam engine, but not so with the rest of the western boys. They had got their mouths fixed up for some turkey & were not to be turned away so easy, but finally, like a pack of dogs, made a grand rally not at all to their credit. The Western troops that are in the Eastern Army are neglected for the Western states send things to the W army & the Eastern states send to their own troops so we get nothin but what our Uncle Sam sells us. But we of the Den (as our tent is called) fared better for we had caught 3 rabbits the day before & had a fine stew, <u>tiptop</u>.

 Charly I should like to be out to Sodus to have spent Christmas & New Years with you. What a jolly time we would have <u>sleigh riding</u>. It is a long time since I have had a sleigh ride & I think if I could get back to the land of snow once more, if I did not have some fun, it would be because Eb was not alive or there was no snow, or <u>girls</u>. But there is no use of me building castles in the air as I am down here where there is no snow or <u>girls,</u> so I will have to bring this note to a close.
 Your Cousin
 Eben Canfield

To Charles and David from father John McDowell:

Dear Sons,   *December 25, 1862*
 We have not heard from you in some time. We want to hear from you much how you are getting along in the war, how long you enlisted for we want now.

 We all wish you both a merry Christmas and a happy New Year and safe return home.

 A lonesome Christmas. We do not lie down a night without thinking about you. My mind is drawing back to bygone days when my little family was around me, but times past never return.

 We are all praying your safe return, both of you, that we may see [you] once more alive. May God bless you.

PART II
1863

Chapter Five
Washington Defenses

January 1, 1863: "President Lincoln signs the Emancipation Proclamation, stating that 'all persons held as slaves within said designated States, and parts of States, are, and henceforward shall be free.' Reactions are, for the most part, enthusiastic. The provisions for freed slaves include assurances that former slaves are to be permitted to serve in the military service.

"Continued difficulties with General Burnside over the after effects of the Fredericksburg defeat still plague the President. After meeting with the chief executive, Burnside states in an open letter that he has felt little support from fellow officers and that he considers retirement in order to 'promote the public good'. Lincoln persuades Burnside to reconsider."
(Bowman, John S, ed. The Civil War Almanac. New York: World Almanac Publications, 1983, 125-126)

To Nancy from Charles:

[Camp Morris]   *Jan the 2-1863*
Dear Nancy,
    I now take the opportunity [to] write a few lines to you to let you know how we are a getting along. We are all well at present except John Perkins. He has a touch of the fever but he is a getting better.
    We have had a pretty good time a New Years. I will tell you what we had for dinner: mashed potatoes and honey that Sam had sent from home, and them pickled peaches, and Bill had these three chickens sent in his box and some fresh pork and some fried cakes [donuts] and some sugar cakes and some head cheese and some good bread. We had all of them things, wasn't that a good dinner? The boys all feels pretty well but they carried on so a[t] Christmas that they won't let them go so much.
    We have drawed our artillery suit and I tell you they are dashy. They are most covered with red stripes and they are made of the first-rate material. We got shoes, socks, caps, shirts, blankets,

drawers, mittens and so on. I thought I would send my other clothes home, they are pretty good and I thought I would go to Washington tomorrow. But Nat I would like to have you come down in February and then you can take them back with you.

Baker's wife and daughter is a-coming down and I guess Len Williams wife. Maybe you know them. They live in Lyons. Baker was a shoemaker there. He works at shoemaking here and Len Williams was a carpenter in Lyons. He is our fourth sergeant. They are nice folks. Baker said if you would come he would write to his folks about it. We can hire a part of a house near our camp and I can have plenty of time to visit with you. I don't know as I can get a furlough next Spring and if I could I would rather have you come down here. I want you to see the country. The cost won't be of much account when you get here. There is getting lots of women here now. The fare on the cars is twenty-two dollars. I wouldn't begrudge that a bit to have you to come and see me and see the city of Washington. Bill says he would like to see you very much.

Letter continued:

Camp Morris   January the 2-1863

I just eat supper. I had some bread and butter and honey. I am on guard today. There is some to work on the fort and some on the barracks and some on guard. I heft to stand two days out of the week. That ain't very hard. I don't have nothing else to do. Our fort is most done and it will be a good one.

Sam Lape is getting better. They make a considerable of fun of him. They say he is so homesick.

Old Mr. Seward was here today. He is a nice old man. He rides in a nice carriage. We shot blank cartridges today for the first out of our cannon.

I went out to a camp where a regiment had left and I got a candlestick and some plates and some cups and some knives so we have got lots of thing.

I remain your ever true and affectionate husband
Goodbye Nat

To Charles from Nancy:

Dear Husband, *January the 2 1863*
We have been cooking some things for you. We are going to send you and David each one a chicken and each a stirred cake and some fried cakes and some butter. We can't send much butter for Stephen has sent for some.

I think that song that you sent was a purty good one. I hope that you had a purty happy New Year. There was lots of balls around New Year. The girls had a time of it. Two girls had to go with one boy.

I heard that the soldiers had the smallpox out there. If was in your place I would go and be vaccinated if they had it. They have got it at Williamson. I hope that it won't come any wares.

I remain your true and affectionate wife.
Goodbye Charly for this time.

To Nancy from Charles:

Dearest Nancy, *January the 4-1863*
I always feel it a pleasure to write to you. I don't think much like writing to anyone else. I feel very sorry to hear that you was sick a[t]Christmas. I hope you are well now. I sent a letter to you day before yesterday but I never enjoy myself more than when I am writing to you.

You say that you feel very lonesome. I know Nancy that you do but you must keep up good courage and live in hopes. Sometimes I feel very lonesome myself but I consider I am better off than a great many. We are in a good place and I think we are pretty sure of staying here till the close of the war. We can't tell when that will be but we think it will end before long but we hadn't aughta to find fault. We have plenty to eat and drink and don't heft to work a quarter of the time. But if you could only be with me Nat I should feel very contented then.

I have been drilling some on our cannon. It ain't near so hard work as I thought it would be. It ain't so hard as infantry. I like it first-rate. We have shot some blank cartridges aready. You would laugh to see some of them drill on them. When they first commence they make some curious moves but they will soon get use to it. They take a thirty-pound ball; they are an ugly-looking thing.

I forgot to tell you how we managed about our candles. I went and got a piece of soap stone and took my knife and made something to burn grease in what you call a slut [?]. We call it a regular bitch.

The other night when I was on guard I came in and it was dark and I was hunting for a match and I tipped it over in Bill's face and I tell you he had a sweet looking face.

We would have candles enough but some of the boys sometimes [stay up] most all night and writes.

From your ever true and affectionate husband

To Nancy from Margaret [Charles's sister]:

Burford [Canada]   January the 4 1863
Dear Sister,
    The receipt of my brother's letter not coming at hand I thought I would pen a few lines to you as I am getting so uneasy. Although you are a stranger to me I am sympathetic with you in your lonesome state. But it is my prayer that they may both return alive and that we may all mee[t] on earth and have peace and unity throughout the land, and that we may be better acquainted than we are at present.

I never thought when I took the parting hand with my brothers it would be so long as it has been. If you write to the boys, send them my love. 3 or 4 sheets of paper would not hold all I have in my heart, so goodbye sister until I receive an answer from you

From your affectionate sister,
Margaret I. Brooks.   Direct your letter to Jesse Brooks. Princeton P.O.C.W.

To Nancy from Charles:

Dearest Nancy,   January the 5-1863
    I received the twenty dollars but I don't want it. You must have made a mistake or else I have maybe. So I guess I will send you the money back. I didn't know as you had so much money.

I am on guard today. It is a splendid night. It is as warm as summer today.

I hear that Axa [?] Winchet and her man has parted again. Sam has had fourteen dollars since he has been here. Some of the boys spends all the money they can get holt of.

I am afraid you didn't enjoy yourself very well New Years.

I remain your ever true and affectionate husband

They are fighting awfully out southwest.

To Nancy from Charles:

The following is an undated letter that I believe was written around the same time as the 1/5/63 letter.

I have just been to dinner. We had fresh beef and beef soup and it was good. I tell you I am getting fat. I don't think your dress would fit me as well as it use to. I never was healthier in my life. John Perkins is about well and so is Sam Lape, but I tell you it's a hard place to be sick.

You say that there wasn't so many killed as they said. There was but you don't hear the correct story. There is twice as many killed as they say there is. We have had another great slaughter but we drove them. I tell you the rebels is tough. The hospitals and the capital and everything else is filled up with wounded soldiers. I was to Georgetown the other day. It's a village that connects to Washington. I was there just after the fight to Fredericksburg. It was an awful sight. Some with their legs shot off and some with their arms off. I tell you it looks tough.

One boy died out of our regiment yesterday morning but they ain't near so sickly as they was a spell ago. There was two brothers died by the name of Alboy [?]. They was a cousin to that Albought that lived at Wayne Centre. They died just a week apart. They had the brain fever. They was crazy.

Levi Dunbar writes to his intended pretty often. I suppose you know who it is when he expects to get a letter and don't get it. He is as homesick as a dog. He will walk up and down the street as though he was crazy.

I remain your ever true and affectionate husband.

Direct to Washington D.C. Ninth foot Artillery Fort Reno N.Y.S.N.Co.D. In care of Captain Lyon.

To Charles from Nancy:

Dearest Husband,   January the 11 1863
You said that you thought that I had lots of money but you are mistaken. I borrowed that of Pa.

They say the reason that Axey Winchet left her man is that he come home drunk one night and three or four boys with him and he catched Axey and pulled up her clothes and showed the boys her t___. I would have knocked him down if I had been [in] her place.

If [I] come out there you won't get rid of me as quick as you did the twenty dollars. I bet you I will stay till you get tired of me and then maybe you can't get rid of me.

From your ever true and affectionate wife

To Harvey Perkins from John Perkins (Charles's tent mate):

Dear Brother,   January 15, 1863
I thought I would write a few lines to let you know how I am a-getting better. I am gaining quite fast. I don't do anything yet.

This is a pleasant place here. I have seen quite a good deal. I have been in service most five months and haint got any pay yet. It is quite a sight to see the forts here and batteries. I haint drilled any in the heavy artillery, yet some of the boys has. Charles McDowell has. He said he likes to drill in the heavy artillery. He likes it better than he does infantry drill.

Ordley is coming down that way to recruit. I don't think he will get many volunteers.
John Perkins

Same letter:
Father,
I thought I would write a few lines to you to let you know that I am trying to make heaven my home. I love the Lord with all my heart. I mean to serve him while I live.

John Perkins was later taken prisoner at the Battle of Monocacy and died in prison in Danville, VA

To Nancy from Charles:

Dearest Wife,   *January 19-1863*

    We moved in our barracks last Friday. We have got things pretty comfortable. Them things you sent came all right. We soon fixed them chickens. Our orderly Carpenter has gone home today. He has gone recruiting but I guess he won't get many but he is as nice a man as they can start.

    I am glad you sent that stamp and envelope for I was out and it ain't very easy getting them here. I wish you would send me three or four. There is a dozen around every day to borrow stamps. We ain't got our pay yet. They say we will get it next week but I don't know how it will be.

    You wanted to know how much it cost to come here and back. Some say from Washington to Lyons eleven dollars and some says 13. I ain't inquired but I am going down in a day or two and then I will know.

    The women feels pretty proud here if they are in the war. You said you was in a hurry for the time to come. I am the same. I would like to have you come right away but we ain't got things regulated right but we soon will have things pretty nice.

    I stand on guard today at the magazine.

    I remain your ever true and affectionate husband

"First One Killed.—The first person in the regiment to be killed by gunshot was a woman, Mrs. Chauncey Hale. She...was detailed as laundress for the company...One morning after Hale had been on guard-duty and had come to his quarters for his breakfast, and while he was yet at the table, the call for guard-mount was sounded; he hurriedly arose from the table and hastily putting on his equipments, his wife assisting him, and as she buckled his belt she gave him a push, saying playfully, "Hurry now, or you will get pricked and put on extra duty for being late." He held his gun in his hands, his thumb on the hammer, and in the same playful manner answered, "Take care or I will shoot you." The gun was a Belgian rifle and went off half cocked, his thumb slipped and the gun was discharged, the large bullet passing through her head, scattering her brains over her motherless children. Hale was nearly distracted with grief. The company had the remains embalmed and sent home. The children were placed in the Orphan Asylum at Auburn, N.Y. Hale was never himself after this sad occurrence, but seemed broken-hearted and despondent. He remained in the service, however, till the end of the war" (Roe 273).

January 26, 1863: General Burnside is removed from the command of the Army of the Potomac and replaced by General Joe Hooker. "Burnside is apparently not displeased with this change, and will assume military responsibilities in the Western Theater...It is hoped by the President as well as by the soldiers themselves, that 'Fighting Joe' will prove to be both able and assertive, qualities which seemed lacking in the sincere but militarily inept General Burnside. " (Bowman 128)

To Nancy from Charles:

Dearest Wife,   *January the 25-1863*
I would have written to you before but I had no stamps without borrowing and I thought I wouldn't do that.
We have had two pretty rainy days but it has cleared off nice. Bill Wager and me went down to Washington yesterday. We had quite a good time. We went all over the city and just before we started for home we took a notion to have our likeness taken. It ain't taken very good. We hadn't quite enough time or we would have had them taken better.
We live pretty well now. We have plenty to eat and drink. There is ten in our house and the way the boys does here when they want lumber to fix anything they go out nights and draw it. Our boys in our tent went out last night and got a nice lot of it. They all went but me. I was pretty tired running round Washington.
Same letter: *January the 27-1863*
It is pretty foggy here this morning. We had a funeral here yesterday. He [the deceased] had a brother that died a few days ago, and day before yesterday, he took chloroform and they couldn't wake him. They didn't know what he done it for.
Some of the boys is down on Lee Dunbar. He was going round the other night with the relief guard and he took one guard to relieve another a little ways off, and while he was gone, the other six run off up to the fort about 50 rods and he reported them and had them put in the guard house and they are down on him the worst kind. But he served them right. I wouldn't be a corporal for anything.

Our fort is most done and it's a- going to be a good one. There is one fort near us that mounts 50 guns. Some of them is two hundred pounders. That would be something to take.

Same letter: Jan the 28 [1863]

I feel very disappointed tonight to think I didn't get a letter but I will wait a little longer. It snow some here today. I feel lonesome going so long without [a letter].

I remain your ever true and affectionate husband

Goodbye Nancy. I hope to see you before long and then Nat we will have a good kind of chat. I spose you have good sleighing out there now. You must try and enjoy yourself as well as you can.

Chapter Six
Nancy moves to Washington

To Nancy from Charles:

Fort Reno *Feb the 3-1863*
Dearest Wife,

I can get a place that would do for you and me but I would rather get in together some way and I think we can have good times here and if you took a notion you might wash for some of our boys. Some of the women here makes money like everything. They get more than they can do. They get six cents a piece and they draw their rations same as we do. But you needn't do this without you are a-mind to. We will see when you get here.

You wanted to know where you could get the money from. I expected to get our pay before this. We expect it any day now but if we don't get it before you want to come, you had better barrow it of your pa and pay him as soon as we get our pay. You had better get twenty-five dollars and you may bring some victuals with you and two or three pounds of candles and you had better bring two bed sheets with you.

Maybe you had better get you a hat, don't you think? That would be better than a bonnet here and you can get you a cloak there or to New York just as you are a-mind to but I think you can do a good deal better to New York.

Wood's wife has gone home today. Maybe you will get homesick before you are here long, but I hope not. I wish you was here now.

We was all vaccinated the other day. They had the nicest machine to vaccinate you ever see. Two could vaccinate a hundred in twenty minutes. They say the small pox is five or six miles off but I guess we won't catch it.

We ain't doing much now. It has been pretty muddy but it is getting quite dry. I hope to see you out here before long and I hope you can stay here till I can go home with you. I would just as leave be here as any place if you are only with me.

Goodbye dearest Nancy till I see you and I hope that will be soon.

To Nancy from Charles:

Dearest Wife,   February Wednesday the 4-1863

Get a through ticket. Start in the morning and you would only heft to ride one night. Miss Wood went home alone. I can get a place for you and me any time you are a-mind to come and the quicker you come, the better because it is healthy now and you would get use to the climate by the time warm weather comes and if you was a-mind to you could get on the cars and be here in a jerk but you can do as you are a-mind to. Come now or wait for company. But if I was you, and wanted to come, I wouldn't wait for any more of them. You couldn't hardly miss the way and when you got to Washington, I would be there to come up with you.

It is nice weather here now. I guess there won't be many passes granted this summer. I don't know but I had better get a pass and go to Canada and see what they are up to there and see if it looks natural. I wished you would send me Margaret's letter to me.

Twenty-five of us went out in the woods today to help load stockades and what do you think we used for plates? They fetched us out a lot of beans and pork and didn't fetch no plates and each of us got a big [wood] chip and piled it full of beans and [we] used a little chip for a spoon.

From your ever true and affectionate husband

To Charles from Margaret:

Burford [Canada]　　　　　　　　　　February the 5 1863
My dear brother Charles:
　　Your letter came duly at hand and was read by me with great pleasure to know that you still returned a spark of brotherly love. I was glad to hear that you was alive and well and your lines finds our the same.
　　I tell you Charly I did not sleep much last night thinking about you. If you had as cold a night there last night as we had here you would freeze to death. Charles I often think of what you must endure, but Charles, I hope there is better times a coming. It is going on 5 years since you left friends and home and if you was to come home now it would seem as if you had risen from the dead. Oh Charles, memory clings to bygone years. I often think if mother was alive how she would trouble about you and David.
　　I don't believe there is a day nor a night but I am thinking about you, but Charles I have got a good husband and a good home. As you say, I am getting the start of you. I have 2 children but I am going to wait till you catch up before I have any more. Charly will be 3 years old in March and Mary Emma was a year and a half old yesterday and 2 smarter children can't be found.
　　Chad and Truman Wand is married, as for John Ennis, he can tell as big lies now as ever he could. I have never been in his house since I was married nor for a good while before. I have got lots of friends now in Norwich but I suppose if we was going down hill they would all be ready to give us a kick.
　　We are going to move next month in Blenhem. Jesse [her husband] has taken a place and if we have luck we will do well there. If this war settles and you come home on a visit, we will go back with you. Jesse thinks he can do better there than here. He often wants me to go to England with him but I don't want to go there.
　　He was to Paris [Canada] yesterday and saw a piece in the paper that the North had got ...Negroes armed for soldiers and that they was sure to gain the day. But I don't believe all I read in the papers.
　　I saw in some of your letters that you sent home that you thought I had forgotten you, but when I go home and see the letters

our folks has got from you and likenesses, it makes me feel bad. Not one of you never sent me one thing and it makes the tears stream down my cheeks when I think of it. You only have got one sister and if you had only sent me a lock of your hair I would [have] been satisfied. You know Charles you always was my confidant and guide after mother died, and Charles it seemed as if all my friends was gone when you went and I believe they was but I ask no odds of none of them but I never will forget you, brother [of] mine, as long as the beautiful sun doth shine. Though absent from home and friends, you be my dark eyed brother. I'll think of thee.

We have not had any sleighing of any [consequence] until today, and it has snowed hard all day and it is snowing hard now.

You said Nancy was going out there the last of this month. I wish I could with her, but if you come back alive, I shall expect you out here right away and what a happy meeting that will be. But if we could only all meet in heaven, that would be still happier. No wars there, nor rumors of wars.

So goodbye dear brother till I hear from you again.

I remain your ever true and affectionate sister Margaret I Brooks.

To Charles from Nancy:

Dearest Husband,   *Tuesday February 5 1863*

I was very glad to get your likeness. I think that it would [have] looked better if you not had quite as much hair around your mouth but I am quite satisfied with it.

David writ that they had the smallpox out there. I want to know if they have got it or not. If they have got it I want to know if you think it safe for me to come out there. They have got the smallpox out here this side of the port. I have been vaccinated today but I don't know whether it will work or not [a mild rash proves that it worked].

Mr. Courtright's folks has heard from David Courtright. He is in Washington now. They don't hear from Alford. They think that he is dead. His wife stole in Lyons the other day. They catched her and was a-going to lock her up. She sayed that she had five dollars. They took that and let her go.

From your ever true and affectionate wife Nancy.

To Nancy from Charles:

Dearest Nancy,   February the 11-1863
    It is as warm as summer here today. You said you was some afraid of the small pox. Well I don't think there is much danger. They said they had it to Washington a spell ago, but I don't hear anything about it lately, but [you] can do as you are amind to about coming. But I don't think there is any more danger here than there is there. I have been vaccinated but it hasn't worked. I am a-going to try it again.
    Me and Dave went out in the country about ten miles. We saw some rich farmers and lots of N___ers. This whole regiment knows Old Miss Drum and they don't give her a very good name either.
    I was weighed this morning. I weighted 162 1/2 pounds. Well I tell you this seems to be a curious place. Some days we lay abed till noon, git up and eat our dinner and like enough go right to bed again. That is when it is wet and muddy and sometimes we eat a dozen times a day. I don't think I will hardly know how to act when I get home.
    I feel some tired of writing. I have wrote five such sheets as this and sent them to Canada.
    From you ever true and affectionate husband Charles
    Goodbye for a while.

To Nancy from Charles:

Camp Morris   Feb the 15-1863
Dearest Wife,
    I was to Washington. There was pretty stirring times there. You would laugh to hear them quarrel in the Senate. I guess they do nothing else there now but quarrel.
    It rained a considerable here last night. The ground had got quite dry before this came on. The boys has had some awful times since they got their pay. They have had the old Colonel up most all night for two nights now to keep them still. He told the boys he wanted them to enjoy themselves as well as they could but he said he thought that they got a notch too high. Well I think they

did myself and they fight in some of the companies and was pretty tough. One fellow from Company I come over to our tent about 2 or three o'clock in the morning and wanted to stay all night. His head was cut up awfully. He said he was afraid they would kill him. He was drunk too, but it won't last long. They about out of money aready and I ain't much sorry.

Here you have a view of our camp before we moved in our barracks. We are moved about forty rods. There was six compan[ies] in these little tents. Two companies had moved when this was taken. You can see that some of them is stockaded and some of them ain't. I will mark a cross on our tent on the left wing so you can see where we lived. This big tent you see is the guard house and where you see these four men sitting down there is the gate and where you see the poll with wreath on there is the colonel's quarters and you can just see a poll near the right wing. That is the hospital. This is taken pretty natural only it don't show the streets quite as they are.

I remain your ever true and [affectionate] husband Charles.

"On the 15th a vigorous temperance movement was made by the captain of Company B, who with a squad of men went out and broke up a liquor hole, where men had been drinking themselves into trouble... For drunkenness all sorts of penalties were inflicted, such as standing on a barrel, wearing said barrel, or another with only the man's head peering through, called a wooden overcoat... (Roe 50-51).

To Charles from Nancy:

Dearest Husband,   *Feb the 20 1863*
I am a- coming [to Washington] with Mr. Traver. We are a-going to start next Wednesday the 25th. We are a-going to take the after noon train. We are a-going by the way of Baltimore. I want you to meet me at the depot. You can tell about the time that I will get there.

I have been vaccinated five times and the last time it made out to work. I don't know whether you will get this letter or not before I get there. If you do I want you to be sure and meet me.

I remain your ever true and affectionate wife.

March 3, 1863 - Congress passes the Conscription Act, which calls for all able-bodied males between the ages of 20 and 45 to serve for three years. A drafted man, however, may pay $300.00 to hire a substitute.

To Charles and David from father John and stepmother Henrietta:

Norwich [Canada]
Dear Children,   *March 4, 1863*
  If I understand you right your time is nearly up in the army. I wish you not to list again by no means. Come away when you can by all means. Do be sure to leave when you can.
  When I write I mean to write to both of you at same time. We long to see you both once more on the shores of time.
  There has not been much sleighing here this winter. Sugar making is just commencing here now. I wish you was here to eat some warm sugar with us.
  We have election here now today. Is the last polling day. We have George Brown the editor of the Globe in the field. It is tight election. I hope the next letter we get you will bring your selves. Charles and David keep out the war when your time is out. By all means come away. Don't forget the reason why I speak so much about your keeping out of the [war] is because they hold out such inducements for you to enlist again. Don't do it. I have conversed with good many people about the [war]. They think it will end very soon.
  Remain your ever-affectionate parents till death.
  John [and] Henrietta McDowell

To Nancy's mother Mary Wager from Nancy:

Dear Mother   *March the 8 1863*
  We had got fixed up quite well. We live in a cloth tent not quite as large as your kitchen. We have got a bed, a stove about as large as my big banbox, that box that Pa got to Ab Warrins for a cupboard. Levi has made me a little table and a little stool and we have got a big one that two can sit on. We have that to sit up to the table with. then I have got wash dish and kettle and a water pail and we have got four tin cups, two knives and forks. We have got

two tin plates, two iron spoons and a candlestick. We have got a bottle of pepersauce. They draw all the vinegar that they want and all the sugar that they want. I have got Billy Wager's teapot. It is the funniest little thing. It has got the spout on the side.

All the boys has been to see me but the baby. He hasn't pluck enough to come.

It has been a raining for about three days.

Charly can draw rations for me so it won't cost anything for me to stay down here as long as I want to. Lieutenants Wads [?]wife arrived here yesterday. She is a-going to stay as long as the regiment stays.

Norman York's wife [is] a- coming back. Lieutenant Regraves has gone home on a furlough and John Shaw at Wayne Center, he is home on a furlough. Miss Fish, she is a- boarding about half a mile from the camp. One of the boys had a letter from Claire Pomeroy. He sayed that they had gone back to Key West Florida. They will have purty hard times in the hot weather there.

Traver he didn't charge anything for the trouble for me a-coming out here and he went down to Washington and got the trunks and Traver and Bill Horn brought it clear up to our tent.

From Nancy McDowell to Mary Wager and Almiry Wager

To Charles's parents from Charles:

Dear Parents,   *March the 8-1863*

I tell you it begins to look like home here since Nancy come here. She arrived here last Friday safe and sound and I was very glad to see her. She thinks this is a curious looking country. She thought it was curious she couldn't see any fences. We stayed out in the country two or three days. Nat thought the folks acts curious out here. She think they are right smart folks. Well we have got right spontaneously situated. Now we have a good tent, a good floor in it and we got a good table and cupboard and bed stand and all such things. I mean good for soldiers. Our teacups are good substantial ones. Nat is learning to soldier pretty fast. She will eat dinner and then lay down on the bed. She said we lived better than she thought we did. Oh we live good.

Oh I tell you this war is a big thing and it is a getting to be a bigger thing. They talk about drafting now. If they do it will make some curious times. They may draft all they are a-mind to and they never will whip the south by fighting.

I don't think the mud ain't much deep here now. The[re] was a fellow that went to go up to the sutlers [army merchant] the other morning. He said he came along where the mud was pretty deep and he saw what he supposed was a man's hat. Well he went up to it and give it a kick and it yelled out and wanted to know what he wanted to be a kicking him for and come to find out a man had got stuck in the mud. It's a pretty big story but I can't doubt it much.

The boys is all well and they seem to be in good spirits. I haven't done much for two or three days now on the count of my vaccination. Give my love and respects to all inquiring friends.

From Charles McDowell

To Nancy from Charles's sister Margaret:

Siddenham [Canada]　　　　　　　　　　　April the 10 1863
Dear Sister:
　　　I begin to feel dreadful uneasy about my far off brothers. I long for to see them face to face and I long to see this cursed rebellion put down. I never thought we should be so long separated when we took the parting hand.
　　　You must feel very lonesome.
　　　Your affectionate sister Margaret Isabel Brooks.

To Nancy and Charles from Almira:

Nancy and Charly,　　　　　　　　　　　April the 30 1863
　　　Ma is been making soap. Pa is grafting trees and Mat is plowing. He has got one field sowed to oats.
　　　We have had one mess of cowslips [a meadow flower/young lettuce]. Lib eat so many it made her awful big. I don't know as I had ought to say anything about cowslips to you. You may want some too. If you do, come and get some.

To Charles and Nancy from Charles's sister Margaret:

Burford [Canada]   *June the 20, 63*
Dear Brother and Sister,

It affords me much consolation to know Charly that your companion is with you. If anything happens, you have somebody to take care of you. It makes me shudder to think of this war, let alone being there, when I read of the wounded laying on the battlefield for 2 or 3 days without being took care of and some lay there till they die for want of care. I tell you if I was a man I would not stand there to be shot at for all upper province.

I was reading the other day about the battle of Vicksburg and it said that the South had gained the day and that they would be sure to whip the North all out. But I hope it is not so, but I do hope that this rebellion will soon come to an end. To think of the many thousand noble men that had left wives, sisters, [and] mothers never to return. But Charles, now you have your wife with you. You must not forget home.

Crops here looks well. We talk of buying this place.

I remain your ever true and affectionate sister Margaret

"June, 1863, is a busy month in Virginia. Hooker and Lee are preparing for Gettysburg, and naturally the forts are hives of apprehension. Diligence is not lacking, and shots enough are fired at targets to enable the cannoneers to become excellent marksmen, if the need arise…on the 3 [r]d all women save those doing company work are ordered from camp…the 23 [r]d Companies D (Charles and David's company) and G…march ten miles to a point near Fort Thayer on the Baltimore & Washington railroad to work on rifle-pits and batteries, three miles from Washington and two from Bladensburg…The men dig ten hours a day, all on account of fear of rebel cavalry that are reported prowling about. (Roe 53-55)

June 28, 1863: Lincoln questions Hooker's abilities and decides to remove him from the command of the Army of Potomac. He is replaced by General George Meade.

July 1-3, 1863 — The North and South sustain heavy losses at the Battle of Gettysburg in Pennsylvania. Lee is defeated and heads back to Virginia. A great victory for the North.

"July, the memorable month of 1863, finds the Ninth at employment no more warlike than the handling of pick and shovel, and filling in the chinks with rilling...many grumbling letters were written home. 'Gettysburg' is on every lip, and the boys remark on their having all the hard work and none of the glory, though they did think there was some chance for them when [J.E.B] Stuart came so near. The women and the sick were sent to Washington, and every preparation was made to withstand an attack. The band was ordered upon the breastworks, and bade play 'Yankee Doodle' for all that they were worth...It was the colonel's idea that music might encourage soldiers as well as charm the savage ear..."(Roe 55-56)

To Nancy and Charles from Almira:

Dear Friends   *July the 5 1863*
  They say the rebels has been within two miles of Washington. I should think you would be scart. Mike Tindall wrote home that Lib was sick. If you get sick you must come home before you get so sick you can't come.
  Pa is very anxious to here from you. He heard that you expect a battle there everyday and he wants to now if you have had it.
  We have quite warm weather here now. The corn grows nice. We have got a few apples yet and they are quite big on the trees. I should not think you would like to live in a tent. They say you have tents now.
  I want you to tell me if Lib is with you now and you may bet that I would not stay there if the rebels is coming in there. Our little Lucy has got to be a big cat and the old cat has had four more and Mat shot them and then Lucy was the baby again. What do you think of that?
  Now I want you to write often and not wait for us, for if the rebs is coming in there we want to know if they have killed you or not, and where you are and how you live.
  From Ma, Pa, Mat, MY and so on and so forth

To Nancy and Charles from Almira:

Nancy and Charles,   *July the 23 1863*
    We heard that Lib [York] was very sick with a fever and had had the doctor and Norm [her husband] had to stay with her all the time. We have to visit the sick all the time, but we are glad that we can do it—that we are not sick.
    We have one lady out here and that is Mike Tindall's wife. You don't now what a swell she cuts. Of all the new dresses, she has the most. Mike sent her home money not long ago. She got it a Sunday and a Monday she went to Lyons and she got lots of new things. They say she don't get his Children anything. Don't let them have anything to eat. More she don't let them have any shirts to wear. I think it is too bad. You had ought to see her bonnet. Lots of flowers and new salls and everything you can think of. The neighbors all say she made his two little boys go without shirts all winter last winter. There is lots of talk about her
    Pa is to work in his wheat. They have to give two dollars a day for hands to work in harvest.
    From us all at home

Chapter Seven
Fort Foote

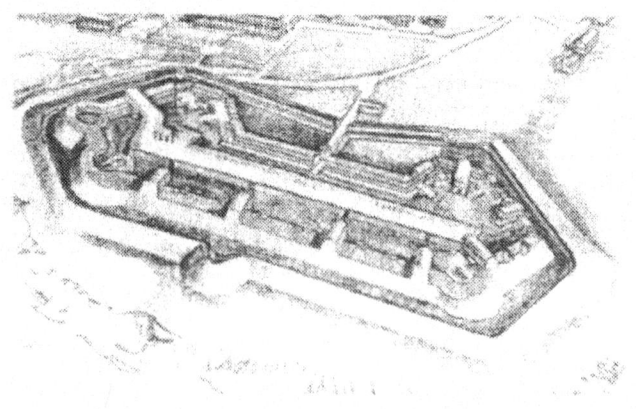

Sketch of Fort Foote courtesy of the National Park Service

On August 14, 1863, companies C, D [Charles and David], E, and G, under the command of Lieutenant-Colonel Seward and Major Taft, marched to Washington and then sailed by steamer twelve miles south to a bluff on the east bank of the Potomac. The regiment was to build a fort on this 100-foot bluff to defend the water approach to Washington. But, "It was a point so unhealthy that it was currently known as the graveyard of Prince George County. Here this command built, with some assistance from engineers, a large, strong work known as Fort Foote. They mounted in it among others several heavy sea coast guns. When these were fired for practice, as they often were, the report shook the surrounding hills as the fever and ague shook the soldiers." (Clark 597).

Even Lieutenant-Colonel Seward could not escape the life-threatening diseases that attacked approximately half of the men. In September, while the young Mrs. Seward was visiting her mother, she received a telegram from the Secretary of State saying, "'William very sick; come immediately with his mother.'...and in a few hours [we]were on our way...there were no sleeping-cars, so we all sat in the hard, straight-backed seats all night...we arrived in Washington early in the morning, so thankful to find our dear one alive, a little better, but desperately ill with dysentery. He was taken sick two days before, and the doctors said that he could not live; sent for his father, who had him carried on a stretcher to Washington, accompanied by his faithful regimental surgeon, Dr. Chamberlain, who never left him until he commenced to get better" (Roe 399-400).

Nancy's time at Forte Foote was spent baking pies and selling them to the soldiers. Apparently she and Charles were rather large suppliers of these delicacies despite the earlier effort to enforce protection "against free trade in pies. The men claimed that this particularly American variety of pastry offered by outside parties was much better than that sold by the sutler, but the edict went forth that it must be the sutler's pies or none. As an immediate result, smuggling of the most heinous character followed, for what freeman could endure having restrictions imposed on pie? Had not Ralph Waldo Emerson said that he rated the intellectuality of a people in accordance as they did or did not appreciate pie? When it came to intellect the Ninth played second to no one" (Roe 51).

To Friends from Charles and Nancy:

[Fort Foote] *November the 6-1863*
Dear Friends,
    I have neglected writing for some time but to tell you the truth, I haven't got much time. I am detailed to work on the barracks and nights, I heft to help Nancy peel apples. Nancy is in the pie business pretty strong. Since she has come here she has made up seven barrels of apples and most two barrels of flour. She has a woman to help her a good deal of the time. She pays her three shilling a day. We sell about seventy pies a day and after payday, we can sell three times that many, if we had them, and we expect that every day now. Money is getting pretty scarce with the boys. We can't tell how long we shall work in the pie business, but as long as we can get things reasonable, we will. If we could get apples as cheap here as we could out North we could do very well, but apples is four dollars a barrel and flour eight and a half and sugar fourteen cts per pound. Lard fourteen cts and everything else high.
    I tell you though I wished you could see our bluff now. We are a-going to have the nicest place you ever see and a very strong place. There was part of a Russian fleet went past here the other day. They lay near at Alexandria. They though[t] of going to the Navy yard but they draw so much water they think they can't run up there. Is four of them. The smallest one draws twenty-seven feet of water. I tell you they look nice. There was a monitor [ironclad] went down the river day before yesterday. We think that the war business looks pretty favorable now but it will be some time yet. In my opinion it depends a good deal on congress now.
    I have traded my old watch off for a revolver and Nancy is practicing on it. She is getting to be quite a marksman.
    From Charles and Nancy

    Mrs. Janet Seward remembers her time at Fort Foote:
    "Fort Foote was the largest and most complete earthwork that was built for the defense of Washington, and I believe is still standing. It commanded the approaches by the river for several miles, and its great guns would make it exceedingly difficult for an enemy to get past it. There had never been such large guns mounted before as it contained, and it seemed to me that the soldiers (it took three or four hundred at a time) would never be able to get them up the bluff and into position. The balls

fired from them were so heavy that I couldn't not even turn one over on the ground, each weighing 500 pounds, and required 100 pounds of powder to fire them. When fired, the men were instructed to raise on their toes and open their mouths to lesson the effect of the concussion.

"One day there came down the president, secretary of war, and several general officers, with their wives, to see the guns fired. Careful preparation and distance measurements had been made for the experiment; a large target placed upon a raft had been anchored near the Virginia shore, about two miles below. The men had practiced until they felt sure of their aim. Just as the party were assembling to witness the smashing of the target with one of the great balls, the colonel was astonished and chagrined to see through his glass a small party of rebels row out from the shore, cut the anchor ropes, and quickly tow the target around a bend of the river out of sight; so the firing had to be made at other objects of an unmeasured distance (Roe 401).

Rodman Cannons courtesy of the National Archives

According to Nancy's obituary, at some point during her stay in Washington, she spoke to Lincoln and shook his hand. This most likely occurred while Charles was stationed at Fort Foote: "Fort Foote provided a varied experience for its garrisons. Visits by dignitaries included President Lincoln and many of his cabinet members. They marveled at the sophistication of the works and the size of the cannon and enjoyed having Secretary of Sate Seward's son and his regiment play host. Lincoln led a party downriver on August 20, 1863...They toured the fort, dined on local peaches and crackers and cheese, washed down with champagne. (Cooling and Owen, Mr. Lincoln's Forts, pp 229)

To Charles and Nancy and from Ma Wager:

Dear friends   *November the 8 1863*
We are sorry to here that Charly is sick. We wish he was at home and both of you was at home.

We heard that you had meetings out there. We was glad to here it. I want you and Charly both to go to meeting and get religion. You are in more danger there than you was here and I think there is more nee[d] of you having religion. It would be a great comfort to you. When I think of your coming home it seems like a long day and I want you to live so that if we don't meet again on earth we may meet in heaven. I want you to think of this.

We are very lonesome here now. We would like to have you here this winter. You must keep up good courage and make the best of a poor bargain.

We have sent you some things. We hope you will get them and they will do you some good.

From your friend Ma Wager

To Charles from brother William McDowell:

Norwich [Canada]   December 4, 1863
Dear Brother,

The present you sent to my dad pleased him very much. The boots and shoes both fitted him exactly and you could not have sent him any other present that would have pleased him so well. He say he is a thousand times obliged to you for it. He feels perty big over them.

Now Charles, I will tell you what I would like to have you do. My dad has bought a nice little horse and he wants me to get another, and I have found one... a three year old colt which is offered for 75 dollars and there haint another as good a one in the county. If you could let me have seventy-five dollars now, and with what I got, it would buy the colt. It will be a-doing me such a kindness that I never never would forget it the longest day I live. If you do let me have the money, I shall call the colt yours till the money is paid back. The colt, I am satisfied, will bring one hundred dollars next fall. I am willing to pay any interest on it that you say, if you do me the kindness to let me have it. I will send you back a receipt immediately or a note payable in October. Now Charles, if you do get the money for me, I don't believe you will ever be sorry for it for I don't say one thing and mean another. Dennis has sold his place for 700 Dollars.

From your brother Wm. McDowell

PART III

1864

Chapter Eight
Nancy Contracts typhoid Fever

To friends from Charles and Nancy:

[Fort Foote]   *January the 10-1864*
Dear Friends,
       We are well at present and enjoying a soldier's life as well as we can.
       Nancy is a- baking pies yet. We have got moved in our new house. It is pretty comfortable. Norman York is a- going home on a furlough and I thought of sending home for a pair of boots. He said he would bring them for me if you would get them, and I wish you would get me a pair and send to me, and I will make it all right with you. I guess you had better get me a good stout hip boot, double soled. Get them quite a little bit larger than this paper.
       I have got to shoulder my old musket and go on guard. I am getting pretty well used to carrying the old thing but our time is passing by swiftly. It soon will be out and then for another years job, but I guess I won't be there. But I find out the longer you soldier, the better they like it. That's the way with our regiment and that's the way with me.
       Yours with respects
       Charles and Nancy

To Nancy's family from Nancy and Charles:

Dear Friends,   *First of February 1864*
       Charly has got his new boots. He thinks that they are too nice to wear. He tries them on four or five times every night.
       You wanted to know if I made pies yet. I think I do. I made 30 yesterday. I made 15 dollars worth last week. That will get me

a sewing machine that cost as much as yourn did, if all is so that I hear.

You say that they are having babies around there. You seem to think that I could have had one if I had stayed at home. I guess I could have one here if I wanted one. There is four women that is a-going to have babies.

Charly is on guard tonight. It is as dark as a black cat and I think it is a- going to rain.

I would like to have about three or four quarts of currants. If you haint got any maybe you can buy some off somebody else.

It rains very hard now. If Mat [Nancy's brother] was here he would want to go up stairs to bed I think.

I would like to know what Mat would do if Chat moved off to the West. He mustn't let her go. They must jump over the broomstick [get married].

From Nancy M Wager and Charly McDowell

Nancy contracted typhoid fever and was sent home to her family's home to recuperate.

To Nancy and Charles from Almira:

Charly and Nancy,   *Sunday the 1[March 1864]*
Ma and Pa went over to Uncle David's and they told them there that Bill had written to them ... Nancy was ...sick.... You [are] to [write] just as quick as you get this and let us know how she is and we think she had better come home when she gets well. She had better of come home with Lib [Norman York's wife] than stayed there and be sick. If she is sick Ma wants her to come home as soon as she is well enough to come home, and she thinks she had better come if she is well. So no more .....

The folks at [home]

To Nancy from Charles:

Fort Foote   *March the 7-1864*
Dearest Wife,
I now take the opportunity to answer your letter that I got the fourth. I thought I would wait till I got your other one. I

expected it tonight but it didn't come. David got one last night. It said you had got home but you didn't feel very well. I am afraid your jaunt has been pretty hard for you but I hope you soon will be better.

After I left you that night I went to a theatre. It was very nice. It lasted till twelve o'clock then I went to the hotel and hired my bed. Had to pay 50 cents. Then I came back in the morning, and in the afternoon, I made 14 pies. But I tell you the old house looks pretty lonesome.

I am to work on the well yet. I stay at the house nights. I haven't been to roll call yet. We had 19 new recruits for our company last night and one came tonight.

Fish expects his furlough in the morrow or next day. I guess I can't send only one trunk. I bought me a nice accordion the other night. I have about sold my big revolver for seventeen dollars and I have bought two shirts off Judd [?]. One of the new ones that we drawed, and one new cotton shirt. So you see I have been dickering considerable.

You had better have the doctor come and see you as soon as you can. What does your mother think about your disease?

From your ever true and affectionate husband C McDowell.

To Charles from Nancy:

Dear Husband,   *March the 8 1864*

I am feeling easy today. The same day that I got home them soars [sores] began to gather and it made me almost crazy. It was gathering three days. I think that it made me some worse a-riding so far. It made some sores than.

I had the doctor the next day after I got home. He said that the fever that I had eased the ulcer in me. He say it most always leaves one so. I hafta take a rubber pipe and run it up my bowels and then take syringe and hafta have it full with [vitriol] and then squirt it up the pipe. I hafto lay with that in my bowels half a day to a time. It has to be applied twice in one day.

I suppose that you would like to know how I got home. I found Mat in Lyons. I rode home on a springboard. When I got home I seen Pa stick his head out and went in again Then Ma, she come. She said, "Wheres in creation did you come from?" They

all think that I have the small pox. I [am] glad they think [that] for [then] they won't trouble [me] until I get feeling better. My [Almira], she ain't very well, so Ma has her hands full.
  From Nancy M McDowell
  You must keep up good courage

March 9, 1864: "U.S. Grant was made Lieutenant General and given command of all the Union armies...President Lincoln had learned that it took a soldier to do a soldier's job, and he had at last found the soldier who was capable of it: a direct, straightforward man who would leave high policy to the Civilian government and devote himself with unflagging energy to the task of putting Confederate armies out of action...from now on the whole weight of Northern power would be applied remorselessly, with concentrated force." (Catton, Bruce. The Civil War, New York: American Heritage Press, 1960, 201)
  Upon receiving his commission and speaking privately with Lincoln, Grant immediately left Washington to join the Army of the Potomac, headquartered in Brandy Station, Virginia.

To Charles from Almira:

Charles,   *March the 10 1864*
  Nant [Nancy] is writing a letter to you and I had nothing to do and so I thought I would write a little.
  You don't know how we was taken by surprise to see Nant coming home. We thought she was well and enjoying her self first-rate but we found we was mistaken when we seen her. She has been pretty sick since she got home but Doctor Harry has helped her finely. She is quite well now but the doctor says she must be dreadful careful or she will get down again. Ma thought if she got well this summer she would do well. Ma makes her keep awful still. You don't now how scart all the folks was. They thought it must be she had the small pox. They would not come in the house and it got all round that she had the small pox. There is a-going to be quite a time a- moving around here this spring
  George Knox was married the other night to Mary Heart. He is forty and she is twenty. The boys had to horn them. Mat was there. He said that Old Knox came out and clubbed them for kill[?].

Pa and Mat is clearing up their new place. Cutting brush and fixing fence. Nant has got a nice little kitty. She has named it Waddy Waddy. I thought that was a funny name.

Almira

Charles was assigned new work at Fort Foote as a result of the following request made by Lt. Col. William H. Seward:

Fort Foote
Feb'y 26th 1864
Lt. Col. J.H. Taylor
Chief of Staff, Dept. of Washington

Colonel,
    I have the honor to state that this Post is at present almost entirely destitute of facilities for landing Troops, Q'Master Stores, Ordnance &c.; the water in the river at this point being so low, that it is impossible for the smallest Tug to land without grounding. Herewith I very respectfully submit plan and estimate for building a Wharf at this Post, should the same meet with your approval, I beg that I may be furnished with a Pile Driver, and the proper materials as per accompanying Requisitions.
    The Wharf is to be built by the men of this Battalion.
I am, Col,
Very resp[ectfull]y
Your ob[edient] servant,
W.H. Seward
Lt. Col. 9th NYA Comm'd'g Post
("Letter Book, Ninth NY Heavy Artillery, Seward House, Auburn, NY.")

To Nancy from Charles:

[Fort Foote]   March the 11-1864
Dearest Wife,
    I have looked for a letter very anxious for two or three nights now but they don't seem to come. I didn't know but you might be worse and couldn't write but if you could I should think you could get some body to write for you but I hope it's not the case.

I am to work at the well yet. We have had 50 new recruits come since you went away. 20 came tonight. Our barrack is getting pretty full. We have all got our houses white washed, privy and all. It looks good. I sent your trunk by David Fish yesterday. I left some of the things in it that you put in and what other things I thought you needed. I sold that big basket tonight to Mrs. Hammond for fifty cents.

They have commenced to build a dock here. It was reported we would get our pay yesterday but we didn't and they say tonight we will get it tomorrow. The N___ers got theirs tonight.

From your ever true and affectionate husband C.

To Charles from Nancy:

Dearest Husband,   March the 15 1864

I am real smart at now. I have had the doctor four times. He is quite surprised to think that I am so smart. I was almost crazy after I got home. My bowels began to gather the same night I got home. Ma, she was scart about me. The doctor said I ought to come home before. He said he thought I would be sick a long time at the least calculation, but I am real smart but I haven't been out doors yet. Ma says I have got to stay three weeks longer in the house. I don't know whether I told you what Harry said caused it or not. He said that it was the fever that caused it.

I don't know hardly what I wrote the other time, I felt so bad. When I get well, if you want me to come back, you must write for me to come for Ma says I shant come back till fall. You can sell the big revolver but I want you to send the little one to me for I will hafto stay alone some of the time. I want that roll of cloth that you found to the river.

They say that Mike Tindall's wife is a-going to have a baby. He won't live with her. They [say] that she says that it is her father that ruined her. George Swift is dead, poor boy.

If you have sent my dirty clothes I will be very glad for I am afraid they will get all rotten. If you haint sent them you can let Miss Hammen to wash my shirts that is stained. You need not be afraid to ask her for she will know what it is. You can pay in some of that dried fruit if you don't want it all.

From your ever true and affectionate wife Nancy McDowell

To Nancy's family from Charles:

[Fort Foote]   *March the 17-1864*
Dear Friends,

    I feel very uneasy for not hearing from Nancy. She said she would write soon as she got home but I haven't got a letter and this is the third letter that I have wrote but I can't hear from there. No way I can fix it. I think it very strange if she is so she can't write I should think some of the rest of you would write. If you knew how I felt I think you would do it very quick but I hope to hear that she is better.

    I feel very down tonight to think I didn't get a letter. If you haven't wrote when you get this, you would do me a great favor by writing.

    From C McDowell

To Nancy from Charles:

Dear Wife,   *March the 20-1864*

    I received your paper with the letter in it and I felt very glad to get it. I begun to think I never would hear from you. It was a good while a coming. I was sorry to hear that you was so bad but I hope to hear in the next letter that you are better. Let me know who doctors you. I want you to get the best doctor you can get. It don't matter what it costs and have him come and see you often.

    I stay in the house nights. I think I shall sell it. I am offered 35 dollars for it. I sold my apples and flour and grease and rolling pin and that little basket to John Dean for 7 dollars last night. They have cleaned the brush and stuff all up of on the hill behind our house. All the way around it looks nice.

    I am detailed to work on the dock. We got our pay last Thursday. I got an allotment and I signed your name to it and Carpenter got the money on it. If you can put it out on interest I will send it home and if you can't I guess I will keep it. Deacon [?] has sold his house. His woman is a-going home this week. He is a-going to the general hospital. There is 18 going out of our company. Our company is full now and more too.

Mrs. Nanitwerts said that Baker's two women told her the reason you went home [is] you was in a family way. She said they said they was pretty sure it was, so she wanted me to tell you on it.

From your ever true and affectionate husband C McDowell

To Charles from Nancy:

Dear Husband,   March Sunday the 20 1864

I am getting real smart for me. The rest is well as usual. I am real weak yet but I don't have to work so I will get my strength. My bowels don't gather any more. They begin to feel natural again. Pa and Ma has gone to meeting. I and My [Almira] hast to stay here alone.

The way that George Dickson paid his three hundred dollars [is] he went around with a paper to get the folks to give him something. Some give him a dollar, and some more, and so they made up the money. Anybody could do as much as that.

You must tell how many pies and fried cakes you have made, and if you stay to the house nights, and all about everything that is going on out there.

From your ever true and affectionate wife Nancy

To Nancy from Charles:

[Fort Foote]   March the 23-1864
Dear Wife,

I feel very much pleased to hear that you are getting better but I feel rather bad over what I think is lost. I sent your trunk by Dave and he got it as far as New York and he didn't get a check there. Dave says he handed up the old check and as he handed it up the whistle blowed and the baggage master ast him if he had his ticket. He said, "No," and he told him to go and get it and by the time he got back he would have it checked and put on the cars. Well, he says as soon as he got his ticket, the whistle blowed and the cars started and he jumped on and didn't go to see anything about the trunk. And when he came to Lyons the trunk wasn't there and he said when he came back to New York he looked for it there but he couldn't find it. I tied a card on one handle with your name on and directed it to Lyon, Wayne County, New York.

It was nothing but carelessness in him. I don't know but it would be well enough to telegraph to Albany or New York. I put all your clothes in it and everything else that was worth anything. It will be a considerable of a loss...

To Charles from Nancy:

Dearest Husband,   March the 27 1864
     I don't get my strength very fast but I think I will get better when the weather gets so I can get out. It is so wet that I can't get out.
     Stephen [Wager] has enlisted again he is home on a furlough [he later loses his arm at the Battle of Cold Harbor].
     You said that you could put it on interest I can get five per cent and maybe I can get seven per cent. Uncle Aloa is going to buy Hank a place and he wants to get some money. If he gets our money we will [get] seven per cent.
     So goodbye for this time.
     From your ever true and affectionate wife

To Nancy from Charles:

[Fort Foote]   March the 29-1864
Dear Wife,
     I have had quite a tramp. I have been gone three days. I went to the old camp and stayed there one night and one night to Washington. I stayed to Old Sniders, and in the night about eleven o'clock, the doctor came in and said they had marching orders. They packed up that night and in the morning, by daylight, they was off. The women felt pretty bad. They shed a good many tears. They have moved just above us.
     I sent to New York for that trunk but it wasn't there. The baggage master says maybe it is sent back to Jersey across the river from New York. Dave don't say much about it. He feels rather ashamed about it and well he might be.
     I stay in the house nights but I don't bake anymore pies. It's too lonesome for me. You say you are lonesome. If you feel any lonesomer than I do you must feel pretty lonesome. Nat I wished you was well so as to be with me for then I wouldn't get lonesome

but we must keep up good courage for I hope it won't be long before we can live together again.
Write soon because I always feel anxious to hear from you. Goodbye my dearest Nancy.

Charles never mentions that on this day his brother David left Fort Foote with a few comrades and stole a rowboat, three hens, and one rooster. According to David's military records stored at the National Archives, he was returned to Fort Foote under guard and charged with absence without leave and theft.

I don't know if Roe is speaking about David, but he writes of this time "As it has ever done, whiskey gets men into trouble…One of the battalion, noted for his love of the intoxication cup, gets drunk, makes a raid into the neighboring country, and winds up his carouse with a musket ball in his leg, sent there by an irate countryman, whom he had most grievously offended. This same soldier was noted for his range of tricks and pranks; he was the man who once smuggled a quantity of liquor out of Alexandria by putting his flasks in a child's coffin and then with a sad face, such as a bereaved father might be expected to wear, he bore his spirits, by no means departed, across the river and into camp" (Roe 63).

To Charles from Nancy's cousin Stephen Wager:

Heron Wayne Co. N.Y.   *April 1st 1864*
Friend Charly
    Dear Sir
        I have a few moments to spare and I thought I would write a few lines to you to let you know that I am well at present and I am in good health and I am at home on furlough. The reason I am at home on furlough I reenlisted for the term of three years more or soon as discharged.
        I expect to go back in about 21 days. I get a pretty large bounty. Three hundred dollars from the county. $800, 50 [?] from the state, 300 dollars from the United States.
        From Stephen Wager to Charly McDowell

To Charles from Nancy:

Dearest Husband,   April the 1 1864

    It is with great pleasure that I sit down to let you [know] how I am at present that I am getting better so I can work some.

    The doctor said that I could not live long as I was. He said that my inwards was all most eat through so I think that if I get well I ought to be satisfied. I guess that Miss Vanatwerp would give all of her clothes if she was well.

    I would like to set eyes on [Fish] again. I would tell him what I thought of him. I believe that he must have sold the trunk. I want to know if he had the key to the trunk.

    So goodbye for a while.

    From you ever true and affectionate wife Nancy

To Nancy from Charles:

[Fort Foote]   April the 2-1864
Dearest Wife,

    John Ost died today. The one they called Wady. The boys all feels very bad. He was a very nice boy. He had measles and he catched cold. We are a going to send him home.

    You said I had better pack up the rest of your clothes and send them there. Is no rest to send of any account only your old dress and some of them old shirts. I had over eighty dollars worth of stuff in the trunk. It's a pretty bad loss but if we can't find it we shall hef to let it go. You say you don't know what to do for clothes. You will haft to go and buy some. You spoke about me sending my money home. Maybe I may send it by Redgrave. I am getting so I am most afraid to trust anybody any more.

    I stay in my house yet nights but I heft to leave it the first of the week. I got two dollars more from Lake on that house at Fort Simmons. I sold it to a fellow in company E for thirty-five dollars. Don't you think I sold it pretty well? That fellow didn't take my big revolver but I can sell it before long. Do you want me to send that little one to you or shall I sell it?

    Write soon because I want to hear that you are well and healthy again so you can come back here and stay with me.

    From your ever true and affectionate husband C.

To Nancy from Charles:

[Fort Foote]   April the 3, 1864
Dear Wife,
    I wrote you a letter last night and sent it in a newspaper and I put a knife in it. I will send one hundred and fifty dollars in the morning by Redgrave. He has resigned You had better send for it as soon as you can. I will send you two fifties, one twenty, three tens. One is the new kind. These fifties draws five percent if you keep them yourself. If you let them out on interest let it out where it is safe. I will send you the small revolver by Redgrave.
    The boys brought down some oysters to my house tonight and we had a good oyster supper. George Helsell is a going home tomorrow on a furlough. He is a- going to take Johnny Ost.

To Nancy from Charles:

[Fort Foote]   April the 6-1864
Dearest Wife,
    I am to work on the dock yet. You wanted to know where the rest of our regiment had moved to. They commence two miles this side of Washington and they garrison nine forts all along down the river. That Walmsy paid that note and I have got my pay for this house. The boys has about all of them paid me.
    I suppose this [is] the last letter that I shall write in the old house. They are a-going to take possession tomorrow. Nat I don't feel like being to home as I did when you was here.
    From your ever true and affectionate husband   [Good]bye Nat for this time, and goodbye old house…maybe forever.

To Charles from Nancy:

Dearest Husband,   April the 10 1864
    I saw Lewd Williams. Says that the Ninth is a- going in a [siege] train. He said that they was going to Richmond. Pa thinks that they the regiment will move. He thinks that I had better stay home till fall but you can tell what you think about it.

I reckoned up our money. There was 520 Dollars. You sent more than I though[t] you would have. [You] ought to have kep some for yourself for I don't want you to be without money.

When I saw Williams he wanted to know if I heard from you. I told him. He wanted to know if you wrote about Dave. I though[t] that Dave must have got in some trouble. If he has I want to hear about it.

I have bought me one new dress. It cost two dollars and half.

From Nancy McDowell to her husband Charles McDowell
You must keep up good courage and I will do the same.

To Nancy from Charles:

Fort Foot   *April the 11-1864*
Dearest Wife,

I am to work at the dock yet.

That man's wife came today that bought my house. Your black dress and your quilted skirt and everything else as I told you that was worth anything much. The lamp I kept, and your old dress and three plates and three teacups and saucers, I gave them to the fellow that bought the house. And some shirts and drawers is about all that is left. I sent you that little revolver. I could have sold it but I thought I would send it to you to remember the Sunny South by.

Our barracks is pretty full now and some of the new recruits is trying to play out a considerable but they don't make out much.

It is roll call. It comes awful early now.

From your husband C McDowell to his wife Nancy.
Goodbye Nat. Be a good girl

To Nancy from Charles:

Fort Foote   *April 16-1864*
Dearest Wife,

There was a dead man floated up ashore the other day. He undertook to run by the parole boat. He was in a little skiff. They hollered to him to stop, and he didn't, and they shot at the bow of the boat. They thought that would scare him so he would stop but he didn't and they took one of their mini rifles and shot him right through the head and he tumbled out of the boat and the tide washed him up a shore. He had one hundred and 54 dollars and a silver quarter.

I am to work on the dock yet.

I have got me a nice little silver. I am a notion to send it home to you. I don't know whether to send my big revolver home or not. That fellow didn't take it as he agreed to. What did they say about you having your hair cut off? Is it a- growing out pretty well?

From Charles McDowell to his wife Nancy McDowell.

To Nancy from Charles:

[Fort Foote]   April the 21-1864
Dearest Wife,

We are going to have inspection today. There is only one woman in company ...that is John Deary's wife but there is lots come in other company. These houses is all full and more too.

You spoke about coming out here if you are well. You can come out here as soon as you are a-mind to only let me know a few days before hand so I can crack us up a little house. I should like to have you here first-rate.

I am to work on the dock yet. Our barracks is getting so full we can't hardly turn round.

From your ever [true] and affectionate husband

To Charles from Nancy:

Dearest Husband,   April the 22 1864

That was purty [mean] for that man to get shot. The poor man wanted to go home. I suppose that he was a soldier. You didn't tell me where he belonged.

You said that you had you a nice little silver and was a notion to send it to me but you didn't tell what it was. Ma reckoned it must be a little woman or else you would told what.

Mike Tindall's wife is as big as she can tumble. Mike won't speak to her when he meets her. They all think it is Leonard's youngone. I heard that they had reduced Sam Lape to the ranks but I don't know how true it [is].

Pa thought I had better let my sheep out to double. I want to know what you think about. Pa thinks they will double in three years. Goodbye for a while.

To Nancy from Charles:

[Fort Foote]   *April the 26-1864*
Dearest Wife,

You spoke about coming out here. I am a- going to put up a house right next to Hammonds. I won't build very large. I can get them stockades that Old Seam[?] got out for his house. I don't hardly think that we will [move]. If we do, I think that we will only move around the defenses. There is two or three more women come.

The leaves is all out here nicely. There was 30[?] of Burnside's troop[s] went down the river yesterday afternoon. Aran Runnels is dead. He died Friday morning. He is a- going to be sent home this morning. He had the congestion on the liver. They expected his father but he didn't come. I am to work at the dock yet. Billy Anson is enlisted in the cavalry and they say they are turning in infantry now.

From your husband C. McDowell to his wife Nancy McDowell

The young Mrs. Seward remembered: "Our tug went once each day to Washington for the mail and supplies. My windows overlooked the winding road down the steep bluff to the river, and we were always interested to see who was coming and going, but saddened when we heard, as we frequently did, the beat of the muffled drum, and watched the solemn procession, marching down to the boat, with flag furled, guns reversed, and slow step, following some soldier who had finished his service for his country" (Roe 403).

To Nancy from Charles:

[Fort Foote]   *May the 1-1864*
Dearest Wife,

We feel sorry to regret the death of Able Dickerson. He died Friday at three o'clock in the afternoon. He had the fever and we think he catched cold about a week before. He was to work on the dock with me. I think he will be started for home tomorrow morning.

I am to work now at building a dock and boathouse for our small boat.

I have got my house up now and all I want is some lumber floor and a roof and it will be but a short time to finish it. It is eleven feet square on the inside and I think you had better come as soon as you can get ready because there is more women a- coming in our company and you had better come before it is full. Write and let me know when you start and I will try and meet you at the city.

I had a talk with Cary and he said he didn't know when he would have his women come. It might be a month and it might be two months. He said he had a talk with his captain and he said that they had their compliment of women now, but if any of them left he would give him the next chance, but he says you mustn't say anything to her about it because he says she wants to come so bad that she will take a notion and come whether he wants her to or not. I wouldn't tell her but what she could come in three or four weeks.

You will heft to fetch some sheets with you if you want any.

From your ever true and affectionate husband Charles McDowell.

Over 130 years later, I visited the ruins of the once great Fort Foote. I trekked down the fort's steep abandoned winding road that lead to the Potomac. There, along the river's quiet edge, I discovered the remains of dock pilings and many large iron nails on the shore. I even found an old rusted screwdriver with the wooden handle worn away. Could that have been Charles's? Was I standing where he had worked, where his dock had received Lincoln on his visits? Where the coffins bearing his friends were loaded onto boats headed back to Washington?

Among the overgrowth I found a well. Perhaps the one Charles had worked on?

Back upon the bluff the huge Rodman guns were still mounted, silently guarding the Potomac. Trees had grown to block their view, for now only the ghosts of fallen soldiers were there to man them

To Charles from Nancy:

Dearest Husband,   *May the 1, 1864*
    I feel very bad [about] the news that I am about to send to you. I am [as] well as I think, but the doctor says I must not come out there till fall, but then I will be out there. The doctor says I will be as bad as I ever was if I come out there in warm weather. But if I live, I will be out there just as quick, as it [is] a little cold, for I am not contented here. You must enjoy yourself as well as you can and I will do the same.
    Joseph Carr writes it is very sickly out there. Ma and Mira is sick. I am the wellest one of us three.
    I hope you won't blame me for not coming, for you know I would come if [I] wasn't afraid of being sick.
    From your ever true and affectionate wife Nancy McDowell

To Nancy from Charles:

                                             May the 2-[1864]
    I am a- going to send today for my lumber. Mr. Hammond and Mrs. Hammond said if you should get here before my house is done we could stay with them a few days but I guess there is no danger but what I will have it finished.
    They are a- going to commence soding the fort today. That will take some time. I reckon when you come to Washington, you go in the room there where you sit because I could find you easier there and if there would be anything to happen that I shouldn't be there, you get on the street cars right near the depot and go up to 19 street and the provost Marshall is there and you get a pass and you get on the cars and come back to the market and get off there and take the next car for the boat landing. The Lookout leaves Washington at ten o'clock in the forenoon and three o'clock in the afternoon, but I shall be there without something turns up pretty bad.
    Let me know when you take the cars at Lyons. You had better take them in the forenoon if you can.

Chapter Nine
Rapidan Campaign
North Anna River/Cold Harbor/ Jerusalem Plank Road

"The Southern nation would live or die depending on the fate of Lee's and Johnston's armies. Grant saw it so, and his entire plan for 1864 centered on the attempt to destroy those two armies...In the West everything would be up to Sherman...When [Sherman] moved, he would go down the Western and Atlantic railroad toward Atlanta; but Atlanta, important as it was to the Confederacy, was not his real objective. His objective was the Confederate army in his front. As he himself described his mission after the war: 'I was to go for Joe Johnston.'

"Grant, meanwhile, would go for Lee.

"Although he was general in chief, Grant would not operate from headquarters in Washington...but Grant's operating headquarters would be in the field, moving with the Army of the Potomac. General Meade was kept in command of that army...But if Grant considered Meade a capable officer who deserved to retain his command, he himself would nevertheless move with Meade's army, and he would exercise so much control over it that before long people would be speaking of it as Grant's army...

"The mission of the Army of the Potomac was as simple as Sherman's: it was to head for the Confederate army and fight until something broke. It would move toward Richmond, just as Sherman was moving toward Atlanta, but its real assignment would be less to capture the confederate capital than to destroy the army that was bound to defend that capital...

"On May 4, 1864, the machine began to roll." (Catton, 204-207)

To Nancy from Charles:

[Fort Foote]   *May the 4-1864*
Dearest Wife,

    Two companies left here this morning. Co. C and E. They have gone to Fort Baker near Washington and maybe you hadn't better come yet. In a few days there is some talk of us a-leaving. We will know in a week or so. I will let you know. I haven't much time to write now for the mail is just going out. Let me know if you sent that money. If you haven't, you needn't.

    C McDowell

Charles will march towards joining Grant's army on May 10th. Prior to that, on May the 4th, "The Army of the Potomac crosses the Rapidan towards Lee, its forces 122,000 strong to Lee's contingent of 66,000 hungry and ill-clad men" (Bowman, 195).

The Army of the Potomac "started to march down through a junglelike stretch of second-growth timber and isolated farms known as the Wilderness, with the hope that it could bring Lee to battle in the open country farther south." But Lee "marched straight into the Wilderness and jumped the Federal columns before they could get across...and on May 5 an enormous two-day battle got underway.

The Wilderness was a bad place for a fight...The woods caught fire, and many wounded men were burned to death, and the smoke of this fire together with the battle smoke made a choking fog that intensified the almost impenetrable gloom of the woods. At the end of two days the Federals had lost more than 17,000 men and had gained not one foot. On May 7 the rival armies glowered at each other in the smoldering forest, and the Federal soldiers assumed that the old game would be repeated: they would retreat north of the Rapidan, reorganize and refit and get reinforcements, and then they would make a new campaign somewhere else.

That night, at dusk, the Army of the Potomac was pulled back from its firing lines and put in motion. But when it moved, it moved south, not north...

Grant had made one of the crucial decisions of the war, and in retrospect the Battle of the Wilderness became almost a Federal victory. This army was not going to retreat, it was not even going to pause to lick its wounds; it was simply going to force the fighting, and in the end Lee's outnumbered army was going to be compelled to play the sort of game which it could not win." (Catton, 207-8)

To Nancy from Charles:

[Fort near Fairfax Seminary?]　　　　　　　　　　*May the 11 1864*
Dearest Wife,

We started yesterday a[t] three o'clock and we marched till half past one o'clock at night. Before we brought up we went over to Arlington Heights and then marched around near Fairfax Seminary. It's a nice healthy place. We have moved in barracks. They are papered off and fixed pretty nice. There was a regiment left as we came in. They had lived here three years and I tell you they throwed away lots of stuff. I got me a new overcoat give to me. I sent you a box of stuff.

I don't know but you had better send me a dollar for I ain't got only two postage stamps and it's hard getting them for I don't believe there is a dollar in the whole company. I never saw them so hard up since we come out.

They think we won't stay here three days. We don't know where we will go. We didn't have anything to eat from yesterday noon till half past one today. Only a little piece of bread apiece but I never felt better in my life. The march didn't affect me a bit but it made some of the new recruits wish they was home.

When you direct your letters direct to Washington D.C. 9th Reg NY heavy artillery Co. D and it will follow us up no matter where we move. We expect every hour to move. A good many thinks to the front but I don't think we will go where it is very dangerous.

That accordion, you will heft to be a little careful with it till it is glued up at the end where it is pulled out some and the keys want gluing fast. Sometime if you are a-mindto take it to Lyons with you. You can get it fixed.

C. McDowell

To Nancy from Charles:

[On the move]   May the 17-1864
Dearest Wife,

I have got a few minutes to write to you letting you know I am well but we are kept on the move all the time now. We start tonight at 10 o'clock for the front but we don't know whether we are going to join Grant or not. We drawed shelter tents today. We have turned in our dress coats and scales [brass shoulder boards used to protect the shoulders from saber cuts] and drawed blouses.

It has been 2 weeks since I have got a letter from you. I think a little curious whether you have neglected or whether it has gone wrong but I should think you could afford to write to me once a week anyway. I wanted a little money but I guess I shall heft to get along without it. I [ain't] got a cent to buy a postage stamp or anything else, but if ever we get paid off again, I think I shall try and keep a little for myself.

I may not have the chance to write again very quick. The boys is all in good spirits and are anxious to start.
    C McDowell

To Charles from Nancy:

Dearest Husband,   *May the 18 1864*
    We heard guns this fore and I think there must be some good news. If you want some money I will send you some for I don't want you to go without any. I should think it was about time they got their pay before they moved them but you can't tell much about war. I am in hopes that they will move the whole regiment nearer Washington.
    Cary wrote that the mail had stopped. If it has, you can't write. So goodbye for this time.
            From your true and affectionate wife Nancy
    It has rained every [day] here for about two weeks and the folks can't do their spring's work.

Belle Plane Landing courtesy of Library of Congress

To Nancy from Charles:

Bell Plane Landing   *May the 19-1864*
    We are at Bell Plane Landing, ten miles from Fredericksburg. There is 10 thousand Rebel prisoners here and

there is more coming all the time but if you would see the wounded come in here you would think our army would be used up in a short time but there is a regiment after regiment coming in here going to Grant.

There is a hill where we have pitched our tents. You can sit here and see nothing but wagon trains and soldiers for miles around. We expect to start tonight or in the morning. We are waiting for the trains to be loaded. Three companies guards a train. One train starts at three o'clock this afternoon. These wagons are loaded with provisions.

These rebel prisoners are tough looking fellows and they look healthy. They ain't dressed as well as our soldiers but they as hearty and well as any of us. I have talked with some of them. They think it will take some time to whip them yet and I think so too.

I don't think they are so bad off as they tell for we heft to cook our victuals now for ourselves but we can get along for that if we only get enough to cook and I guess we will get enough of that. We cook our tea and coffee in our cups and fry our meat on our plates. We don't get no more soft bread. It's hardtack but we like it very well [looks and tastes like a very large, hard, saltless saltine cracker]. Grant is still fighting yet but I think that there will [be] a pretty hard time before they get Richmond. We expect to heft to help take it. We may have a hard time but we will heft to run our chances.

We have got to put up six days rations in our haversacks.
From C McDowell to his wife Nancy McDowell.
We have just got orders to strike our tents and leave.

"We were not to march hungry nor unarmed, for all started away from Belle Plain with six days rations and forty rounds of cartridges, quite a load in itself. ...This going to the front was a new experience to most of the men, and it did not take long to lessen the baggage which the special order had named as necessary. Hundreds said, "If we only had these blankets at home, how nice it would be, but they are a nuisance here," and off they would go from the knapsacks...In their extremity, some men threw away, at once, knapsack and all it contained...If those in authority had only told us what we really needed and what we had best leave behind, how much better it had been for all; but the mere waste of property was of small consideration..." (Roe 83-84)

To Nancy from Charles:

(Milford Station, 30 mi. from Richmond) May the 24 1864
Dearest Wife,

We are at Milford station 30 miles from Richmond.

We marched all day yesterday and all last night. We are driving the rebs before us like sheep. We expect to fight some today but we feel first-rate. Some fatigued. The houses and railroad here is all torn to pieces. The women is crying and they feel bad. They can't get nothing to eat. We left Dave [Charles's brother] at Bell Planes. He was sick and sent back to Washington

Sent[d] me some stamps when you write but don't send money for I may not get them. I ain't [got] no more time to write for we are packing to leave. We are going to chase Old Lee. I hope we will soon whip them out but they are tough. We passed Grants headquarters they are...[rest of letter missing].

Seward Promoted:
"The 24th of May beheld us again advancing, but at 9 A.M. or thereabouts we were halted, and Colonel Seward took formal command of the regiment, announcing that Colonel Joseph Welling had resigned and that he, William H. Seward, Jr., had been promoted to fill the vacancy. His address was not long, but it was direct, and all felt that there would be no flinching, so far as the head of the column was concerned. We are enjoined to do our duty faithfully and manfully, and then came the "Forward, march!" for the first time from Colonel Seward."(Roe 88)

"On the 25th the regiment crossed the North Anna [River] and formed a line of battle confronting the rebels and becoming a part of the Army of the Potomac. The Ninth was cordially received but with rather a free use of such terms as 'Washington Gunners,' 'white-gloved soldiers,' bandbox regiment,' etc., etc. (Clark, 598).

To Charles from Nancy:

Dearest Husband, May the 25 1864

I now sit down to answer your letter that I received tonight dated 13 [?]. I was very glad to hear from you but was very sorry to hear that you was going into battle, but I live in hopes that you will come off unharmed. But the Lord only knows.

I have written you six letters within two weeks, but you don't tell whether you get them or not. I have sent you two dollars in money. I would like to know wheth[er] you get it or not.

I have been to Alton tonight and it rained awful hard, but I got a letter and that paid me for all my trouble. And it would [have even] if I had got half drowned.

We haven't heard from Stephen [Wager, Nancy's cousin] since he went away. We don't know but he is killed but I hope not [he would soon fight in the Battle of Cold Harbor with Charles].

I am very thankful that you keep well and would be more so if you didn't haft to go in to battle. But if it is to be it can't be helped, but hope that there hasn't been any ball made to kill you yet.

We haven't got the last box from Lyons yet but Pa is a-going down in a day or so after he gets his corn all planted. There is a-going to be lots of fruit I think. The trees is all put out full. You must write often as you can get a chance if it is every day. For I do [like] to hear from you so.

I remain your ever wife Nancy McDowell
Goodbye for this time

"On the 26th, the regiment was assigned to the Second Brigade, Third Division, Sixth Army Corps; the brigade commanded by Colonel B.F. Smith of the One Hundred and twenty-sixth Ohio; the division by Brigadier General Rickets, and the corps by General Wright. Now commenced a rapid march for the Pamunkey River and thence to Cold Harbor, where the corps arrived June 1st. On the march there was some heavy skirmishing and the Ninth took its full share as flankers and skirmishers..." (Clark 598-599).

To Charles from Nancy:

Dear Husband,   *May the 31 1864*
We hear great stories from the Ninth. I heard a Sunday that it had been in battle and there was nine killed and _____ght wounded out of company D but I did [not] believe it but it makes me feel very bad for fear it is so. I heard that Norman York [their good friend] was killed. Mike Tindall's wife has got her baby. It's [a] few weeks old. Mike won't go near her now. He won't speak to her.

The folks think the war will end this fall. I hope that it can for I want you to come home. Dave thinks that he will come home [on] sick furlough. It will seem purty bad for Dave to come home and you hafta stay there.

Lib York's [Norman York's wife] baby is the littlest baby that I ever saw. It is so poor it don't look a bit healthy. I don't think that it will live long.

I want you to write just as often as you can get a chance because I want to know if you're are alive. Well, goodbye.

From Nancy McDowell to dearest husband

But Lib York's baby did live; though Norman York would never see his daughter. He died in prison after being captured at the Battle of Monocacy. When the baby became a mother herself, Roe, also taken prisoner at Monocacy, visited her and expressed how desperately her father had wanted to live to be with her.

Nancy's letter continued:

Dearest Husband,   *June the 1 1864*

I thought I would write you a few more [lines].

Pa went to wash sheep yesterday and we all went with him. [We] went down to fish and I fell into the bay. Bill Alvord he helped me out. You better believe I got a good ducking. Ma though[t] that I got fisherman's luck.

To Nancy from Charles:

Near Cold Harbor   *June the Sixth, 1864*
Dearest Wife

I now take the opportunity to write a few lines to you and I feel very thankful that I am alive to do so.

We have been fighting for most four days. We was relieved about three hours ago to come to the rear and rest a little but we have been for three days where we doesn't stand up a minute without having a dozen bullets sent at us. They are having an awful fight here. The first night we came here we charged on them and took eleven hundred prisoners. Some of the boys was so excited when the rebs jumped upon the parapet and held up both hands, they fired right in them. We charged on them day before yesterday and took one line of breastworks but we lost a good many men. They mad[e] a charge on us but they got handsomely repulsed but they fight well.

We haven't lost many in our company yet. Haw was killed yesterday laying behind the breastwork. Byscent Luchese was wounded so we don't think he can live. The rest ain't mortally wounded. Wesley Burns is wounded. George Clump, Mike I Heart, William Burt was wounded slightly. Company C, I think, has lost the most. I think it's thirty-seven killed and wounded.

Oh this war is an awful thing. We didn't know anything about it at Washington but we have been on the move night and day ever since we left Washington. We heft to cook our own grub. The boys is all as hearty and as healthy as bears and feel in good spirits.

When we was on the march coming down here, I used to feel sorry for some of the women. They cried and went on awfully. They boys would shoot their cattle and chickens and pigs and everything else and go right in the house and take anything they wanted.

We are getting our cannon and mortars planted. I think we will give them same thing that they say...

We have got them about surrounded. They have got one pretty bad piece. They shoot railroad iron in it. It makes pretty bad work. They call it seven miles from here to Richmond and I expect we shall heft to fight the whole way.

Our colonel, I think, showed himself pretty small. I should think he would be ashamed to show his head where he is known. But Colonel Seward shows himself a man, not a coward. In the charge he went right in. He took one rebel with his sword and knocked him head over heels and he got one leg of his pants tore most off on him. He looked pretty rough. I tell you it fetches these officers right down. Sam Lape ain't been with us since we first come here, whether he has skedaddled or where he has gone, we don't know. We saw Sam Toursam. He is well.

I would send me a paper once and a while. We don't get such a thing here.

We belong to the Sixth Corps Third Division Second Brigade.

I hope they will give us some chance to sleep some tonight.

From you ever true and affectionate husband

Vanderbelt was shot right through the under arm. It's pretty bad. Hank Porter was just shot dead. I help carry him out.

Young Mrs. Seward remembers that her husband was appointed Colonel, "receiving his commission just as he was going into the battle of Cold Harbor. We did not hear from him for weeks. After dinner I always went upstairs and stayed while the nurse went to her dinner. On the evening of the 1st of June, while sitting in the twilight, I heard my Husband call 'Jenny.' I jumped up, listened, and heard again, 'Jenny,' so distinctly that I went into the hall, and again came the voice, 'Jenny' so plain I looked over the railing, fully expecting to see him coming up the stairs. There was no one there, and I went back disappointed, thinking how strange it was. Afterwards, I found that this occurrence took place at the very hour that he was in the Battle of Cold Harbor, and came very near losing his life" (Roe 405).

Perhaps Charles didn't know it at the time, but on the 3rd, Nancy's cousin Stephen Wager was hit in the arm by a minie ball and his arm required amputation at the shoulder. He would never regain his strength after the amputation. When visiting Cold Harbor over 130 years later, I found a small portion of the battlefield still visible as well a house that once served as a temporary hospital for the Union. It was noted on a marker that the owners of the home moved to the basement while the amputations were performed above. Blood seeped down to them through the floorboards.

Despite Charles's successes on the 1st, 2nd, and 3rd, Grant's major frontal assault beginning on the 3rd is a disaster.

June 3, 1864 - "It begins at 4:30 in the morning, countless thousands of Union soldiers rising from their entrenchments and marching straight toward the fortifications of the enemy. Then 'there rang out suddenly on the summer air such a crash of artillery and musketry as is seldom heard in war.' The dead and wounded fall in waves like mown wheat. For a short time the Confederate breastworks are reached, but then a murderous countercharge sends the Federals back.

"Within the space of a half-hour 7000 Federal troops are killed and wounded, their bodies blanketing the ground before the enemy breastworks...'The groans and moaning of the wounded, all our own, who were between the lines, were heartrending...

"Grant will observe in his memoirs: 'No advantage whatever was gained from the heavy loss we sustained.'" (Bowman, 207)

Meanwhile, during the days that Lee and Grant remained in close contact at Cold Harbor, on June the 8th, "By a large majority Lincoln is nominated for President...The party platform calls for reunification, pursuing the war to its end, no compromise with the South, and a constitutional amendment forbidding slavery." (Bowman, 208).

June 12, 1864: "Grant made his final move--a skillful sidestep to the left, once more, and this time he went clear across the James River and advanced on the town of Petersburg. Most of the railroads that tied Richmond to the South came through Petersburg, and if the Federals could occupy the place before Lee got there, Richmond would have to be abandoned. But General William F. Smith, leading the Union advance, fumbled the attack, and when the rest of the army came up, Lee had had time to man the city's defenses. The Union attacks failed, and Grant settled down to a siege." (Catton, 211-13)

To Charles from Nancy:

Dearest Husband,   *June the 15 1864*
I heard the other day that you was wounded but I hope that it isn't so. I was up to Alton the other day and heard the names read over of the killed and wounded. I expected that your name would come next but it did not come. You better believe I was glad for then I though[t] that you was in the land of the living.
But I think that it is strange that I can't hear from you. They all tell about getting letters but I can't get any. If you get hurt I want to know it and I want to hear from you [anyway]. I think sometimes that you are sick [is] the reason [I don't hear from you] but I hope that you are not sick or wounded.
They say that Stephen Wager has lost his right arm in the last fight. They say that Bill Burt was wounded.
I am going to Alton tonight and if I get a letter tonight, I will think that I will get paid well for my walk.
From your wife Nancy McDowell

To Nancy from Charles:

[Near Petersburg--City Point?]   *June the 19-1864*
Dearest Wife,
I now take the pleasure to answer your kind and welcome letter and I was very glad to hear that you are well and I feel thankful that I am alive and well to answer your letters. I got three

letters from you last night and I felt very glad to get them. I got your letters with one dollar in each.

We are now near Petersburg near the James River. We have had some pretty hard marching. We haven't had a good night's sleep since we crossed at Fredericksburg, but we all are pretty tough and you would think we looked tough if you would see us. Our buttons and guns don't shine much.

I tell you a soldier's life is a curious life. Sometimes we are ordered to halt and put up our tents and we just get them up and we are ordered to pack up and leave. It ain't once but very [often] the case when we stop we ain't sure of stopping five [minutes] in a place on some of our marches. When we would stop I have seen some of the men drop right down in the middle of the road. They would be so tired and sometimes the dust flies so we can't see a rod ahead of us and it isn't a very good place to get water. We heft to go pretty dry sometimes. I have went a mile lots of times after water. When some of the folks at the North thinks that [we] ain't a-doing nothing, I wished they was here and had some of our marches. I think they could go have and take a good sleep and be satisfied.

We was ordered to make a charge yesterday morning at two o'clock but we got in front of their works and we found them rather strong and we had to fall back. They sent a few bullets after us but none happened to hit us.

John Dean was shot through the head when going out of the pit to make some coffee. He died instantly. John Dennis and Davy May Cartly both of them was shot through the head by the rebels sharp shooters. They are pretty good marksmen.

You know we have always heard that they was almost starved out but that is played out. They have got plenty to eat. Them prisoners that we took at Cold Harbor, their haversacks had plenty of hoecake and some had ham in and a good many of their canteens was full of whiskey. We had a flag of truce hoisted twice when we was there to have a chance to bury the dead. We would go half way to meet them and change newspapers and they talked very reasonable about the war. They say if it wasn't for the officers that they would be all right. They are as tough and as hearty looking set as you would wish to see. I have had some of their hoecake. It is first-rate. I would rather have it than to have our bread.

Our gun boats lays here within shelling distance of each other, but our boats doesn't run up to them for fear of the torpedoes. They have the river full of them. One of them had nineteen hundred pounds of powder in it. The way our folks does, they get some old scows (flat-bottomed boats) and get them a- going and let go of them and let them run against their[s] and that makes them go off.

We can see the rebel train of wagons across the river from here. We are a- going to have some awful hard fighting before we get Richmond yet. As the rebs says, we will find the hardest road we ever traveled and I think it's about so.

I don't have a chance to write very often cause we can't get a chance to send them unless we come across these Christian Commissions. I did not put them postage stamps on that letter. They must have put them on. I didn't put stamps on any of them only the last one I sent.

They say you can draw five dollars a month from the first of March. You want to go to the town. They say any man that has got a wife, she can draw it. I have seen some here that said their women got it.

We have just moved ten miles since I started to write this today. We have moved so we can see Petersburg. They throw a few shells among us once and a while. There was a regiment's time out and they got all packed up ready to start and there was a shell come along and killed one man dead.

I expect we shall have a hard battle here. We can shell the town all to pieces in 2 hours but they don't want to do it.

From your ever true and affectionate husband C McDowell
You must keep up good courage.

To Charles from Nancy:

Dearest Husband,   *June the 22 [1864]*
Sometimes I think that you're sick or dead or else I would hear from you. All the boys has written home but you and John Perkins, and they did not write anything about you. I am at Samuel Lape's today to see if she [his wife] could tell anything about the regiment. She says that Samuel is not in the regiment. He is sick. He has got the fever.

We heard from Dave the other night. He is real better. He is in a hurry to join the regiment but I think that he is foolish. I would stay as long as I could.

Stephen Wager got his arm shot off. They amputated it in the shoulder joint. I don't think that he will get over it. I think that it will kill him.

Tonight is mail night. Oh if [I] can get a letter tonight I would be dreadful glad, but I will hafta trust to luck.

From your every true wife Nancy McDowell

To Nancy's father Charles Wager from JW. Westfall:

Washington DC.   June 25, 1864
Mr. Charles Wager
Dear Sir,

I wrote some time since a letter to Mr. Stephen Wager's father apprising him of the situation of his son - where he was and how to address him. His arm having been amputated in the shoulder socket and started bleeding twice after - and - I thought he could not live and wrote you accordingly. He rallied afterward and is now improving weekly. Expects to be transferred to a northern hospital soon.

He is anxious to hear from home and thinks you have written directing it to the Reg't & c- and the home message has gone down to the front with the army mail. Leave off all else and direct simply to:
"Armory Square hospital
Ward M-
Washington DC.
and it will reach him direct. He desires me to write to his uncle this time as you live much nearer to office than his father. With his kind regards to you all.

I am Respectfully yours JW. Westfall
                    Washington DC

The Battle of Jerusalem Plank Road, Weldon RR

To Nancy from Charles:

(Near Petersburg. This letter was written on the available space on Nancy's letter to Charles dated June the 15 1864)

Dearest Wife,   *June the 25-1864*

    We have just been relieved from the skirmish lines. We have been on three nights and three days which we ain't slept. I don't think we have slept three hours in the time and we feel some drowsy but I washed my shirt and drawers.

    We made a charge on the rebels night before last and drove them about a mile and a half. I tell you we made them run. We started about sundown and we charged right through the woods till dark and our line got a considerable broken and we had to stop and I think it's well we did. We was only a mile from the railroad and if we had got there they might catched us. They charged on us [to]night and took their ground back again and took some prisoners but I don't think they took any from our regiment. I hear they have wounded a few from the Ninth. They charged just to the right of us. They came on us by the left flank in three columns and if they had only knowed it they could have gobbled the whole of us all up but we swung round and they doesn't hardly venture but we have drove them back to the railroad.

    The order was passed down our lines last night that Burnside had took Petersburg yesterday fore noon. There was awful heavy firing there. We lay about four miles from Petersburg.

    It's getting very warm here now. You had aughta to had seen us the night we charged on the rebs. I don't think there was a dry thread on any of us.

    You think Nat I don't write to you very often. Well I know I don't and I am sorry. It's so I can't write a little oftener but I couldn't send them if I had them wrote but I think we can send them from where we are now better. I am scarce on paper and envelopes. I don't know where to get an envelope to send this. When you write send me a sheet and an envelope in it till I get some place where I can buy some. I don't think there is ten cents worth of paper in our whole company and they can't get it now.

The captain had a letter from Sam Lape. They think he rather played out. They will be apt to try him some when he comes back.

I haint had a letter from Dave in some time. I don't know how he is. Let me know if you hear from him.

From your husband C McDowell. Goodbye Nancy for this time.

You needn't send any paper now. I bought some tonight. A peddler came in. I had to pay 40 cts for a package of envelopes and paper. Is high too. We talk of moving tonight. Fredericksburg isn't taken yet.

To Charles from Nancy:

Dearest Husband,   June the 25 1864
I now sit down to answer your kind and welcome letter and was very glad to hear from you. Oh yes I had almost give you up but the welcome message come at last. It is all I ask for in the world that your life may be spared so that you can return home to your loved ones. I think that I would be happy then. I don't think that anything would make me unhappy whe[n] I could have you so near me and know that you wasn't in such great danger that you are now in. But the lord knows best whether I shall ever see you again or not.

I think that your letter has been a [good] while a-coming. It was written the six[th] day of the month and I got it the 24th day of the month. I thought that I would tell you for maybe you would think that I did not answer soon as I might but I don't want you to think I would do so for I intend to write to you and see that it gets to the office whether I do anything else or not

You wrote that you did not know where Samuel Lape was. I saw his wife the other [day]. She said that he was sick with the fever and was picked up with the sick and wounded and was carried off the field after the battle was over.

Stephen Wager was in that battle and got his right arm shot off and had it amputated in the shoulder joint. We heard that he was dead, but we don't know whether it is so or not, but I hope that isn't so. I hope the lord will spare his life so he can come home. He is one good boy. He ain't the same person as he was when he went away in looks or actions. He has grown wonderful. He is bigger than Brother John was when he went away.

Axy Winchel has got home. She went to Michigan to live. She stayed just three months and then come home. I think that she is the awfulest girl I ever saw. She don't care for nobody if she can have her way. Miss Cary don't hear anything from her man as he can't write and I think that the rest has all they can do to write for themselves and not for him. She thinks that he is wounded. They had the story around that he was.

It is awful dry here. Everything is dry ____ up but it looks as if it was going to rain. It has been about five weeks since it rained.

Alice Wager is married. Sam Shannon went with her when he was home. She has got a good man they say. His name is Lewis Sober.

From your ever true and affectionate wife Nancy McDowell
I bid you goodbye hoping to hear from you again.

I wish that I was there to cook your gruel for you. I would think it a great pleasure but I can't so we will hafto put up with it.

To Charles from Nancy:

Dearest Husband,   *June the 28 1864*

Bill Dunbar was buried yesterday. He is William Anson's father. He has been sick five or six years. If William Anson is there you must tell him that his father is dead, and if he isn't there, you must tell me in your next letter for his mother wants to know.

I want you to tell me how much Dave pays towards the boxes. He had almost as many things as we did but that don't make any difference. I want to know about it. You said that he was to pay half of the freight but he says that he pays half for one box. I don't think that is hardly fair.

From you true wife Nancy McDowell

To Nancy from Charles:

[Near Petersburg]   *July the 1-1864*
Dearest Wife,

    I now take the opportunity to answer your kind and welcome letter and was glad to hear that you are well. I feel very glad I am alive and well to answer your letter.

    I got your letter day before yesterday and I meant to have sit right down and answer it but we have been on the march so I haven't had a minutes time till now, and we stopped here about two o'clock this morning to rest till day light. We expect every minute to hear the order to fall in. We have been down about ten miles from Petersburg tearing up the railroad and building breastworks and now we are back. We burnt a station and a train of cars.

    You had better believe our boys looked into them houses. Some going there and back. They don't go in a house and ask if they may have them but if they see anything they want, they take it. I got a good quarter of bacon and some flour and I had some pancakes and we lived well but I feel sorry for some of the women. They will cry and beg awfully but it don't do no good.

    It's the most fun to hear the wenches. It was laughable to see them the other day. I don't know but I told you about it but it's good enough to tell of again. We [were] near an old Richmond farmer. He had a large gristmill and a good many out buildings. Well he had a good many wenches around him but his N___ers had left. Some of the boys would go in one part of the house and commence taking stuff and the women would run there and try to get them [the goods] away from these[men] and when they [the women] was there, the boys would break in another place and then they would run there. And a couple of boys got a pig and a N___er wench run and said that was hers, and she got hold of it and pulled back and the boy pulled the pig and wench along for quite aways and then they let go and let her take it back, and while this was going on some of the boys was in the mill and they got it to running, and you had aughta to have seen [how] the old man went. Oh we had lots of fun there.

    I wish when you wrote again you would send me a chunk of camphor gum in a letter or in a paper and I don't know but you had better sent me a few stamps. I don't know as they go through without. I am a-going to put one on this letter, one that you sent me. You can't get a stamp here for love nor money.

Sam Lape stretched the story if he wrote as you say. John Perkins says he has wrote but couldn't get no answer. What is wages up there now? It is awful warm and dry here now.

You was saying you would like to be here so as to cook for me. I wish it could be so. I shall feel thankful if I can get home so you can cook for me. I shall feel well satisfied for that. And I don't know when that will be, but time will only tell.

From your ever true and affectionate husband C McDowell
Goodbye Nancy.

To Nancy from Charles (written on Nancy's June 22nd letter):

Perhaps near Petersburg in a confederate home
Dearest Wife,   July the 4-1864
I ain't where I was last fourth but... we have got a nice place here for a day or two.

There is two women lives here. An old woman and a girl, and they cook for us and we fare pretty well. Her man was drafted out for thirty days to help defend Petersburg and he got wounded. This woman was in Petersburg two weeks ago and she said there was lots of women there. Now I have got a table to write on now and a chair to sit on, something that I haven't had in some time before.

But the folks is in some danger here. There was two balls come the other day and went through the window. It made them look wild. The soldiers before we guarded the house came before they was up and broke in the house and took everything they had. They was left without a thing to eat. I don't know what she would do if it wasn't for the [our] soldiers. They give them hardtack and coffee. I don't know what the northern folks would say if the soldiers would come through there and serve them as they do here. I'll bet you they would be mad enough to bite their lips.

It only takes about one day to use up the fence on one farm to make coffee and cook by. And it don't matter whether it's a board fence or a rail fence or the boards off on the barn, it's all the same.

We draw fresh bread now twice a week. I eat a whole loaf for breakfast this morning. I made some flour gravy and the woman give me some greens made out of cabbage and one thing another and it went real good and it's about noon now and I must go to cooking again.

I got a letter from Dave. He said he was coming here pretty soon.

From your husband C McDowell to his wife Nancy. Goodbye Nancy. I wish I was with you today.

Charles letter continued on Nancy's letter dated June the 28th:

I will now write a few more lines to you. The fourth is past. I enjoyed myself very well. That woman cooked me some more greens and they was good. If it wasn't for one thing I would be most a tempted to strike up a bargain with the girl. She is a real nice clever girl. I got the paper last night but if I was you I would[n't] send any letters in a paper because if I ain't there when they come, the boys opens them.

Bill Anson is here. He wants to know where his father is buried. Them boxes of things that was sent: Dave pays according to the stuff he sent in them of course. Did that box come with the two overcoats in and how much did it cost? Did that accordion come through all right? ---do you like it?

Let me know if you have been to the county supervisor yet. John Albok says his wife got the money.

If you have got fifty cts or a dollar I wish you would send it to me and a postage stamp now and then. I want to buy a little flour to make a little flour gravy once and a while.

We had to keep awake all night last night. We expected to be attacked but wasn't.

From your true husband C McDowell to his wife Nancy

To Charles from Nancy:

Dearest husband,   July the 5 1864

I would like to know how you spent the Fourth of July. I did not enjoy it as well as I did last Fourth and you know about how I spent last Fourth.

I went to a Sunday school celebration but I wished myself to home. I saw some soldiers there on crutches. They make my heartache to look at them. They was out of the Hundredth Eleventh Regiment. It seems real cruel to see so many young men cripples. Jon Cary has got wounded in both hips. They think that his soldiering is at an end.

It is very cold and dry for this time a year. I sold all of my wool. I had six dollars and half worth [of] wool. I got me a new pair of shoes. They cost thirteen shillings. Pa is plowing his buckwheat ground. It is so dry that he can't hardly plow it.

They say that Stephen Wager arm isn't took off in the shoulder. They say that it is between his elbow and shoulder. That is good deal better. He is coming home as soon as he gets able to come.

I heard that Sam Lape was dead but one can't tell much by what they hear. I would like to know if you knew anything about him. We had a letter from Dave. He says that he is almost well. I guess he ain't in such a hurry to come back to the regiment as he was before. He did not say anything about it this time.

They say the women that is a-suffering, they can draw five dollars a month. That is what they say around here but I can't get Pa to go and see about it. He is afraid I will get it. He says there is no use of such a law. I can't think any more.

From your true wife Nancy McDowell to Charles McDowell

Chapter Ten
Battle of Monocacy
Also known as the "Battle That Saved Washington"

Lee sent Jubal Early and 14,000 men through Shenandoah Valley to Maryland to capture Washington, D.C. General Lew Wallace (who later authored <u>Ben Hur</u>) hastily pulled together an army of 6000 men, the New York Ninth included, to confront the Confederates at the Monocacy River (approximately forty miles north of D.C.). He knew defeating them was impossible, but he hoped to buy critical time to allow Washington to prepare itself.

To Nancy from Charles:

[Washington area]   July the 18-1864
Dearest Wife,
    I feel very thankful that I am alive to write to you once more. But we have had some pretty sharp work that day that I wrote to you. We went to Frederick and commenced fighting and we kept it up most all day when we had to fall back. There was too many of them for us. Our company is pretty small now. There is a good many killed and wounded and missing and I can't tell you who all was wounded now for there was a good many left on the battleground. We had a pretty hard march that night. We marched eighteen miles. You had aughta to have seen the Hundred Days fellows [men who enlisted for 100 days] skedaddle. They throwed their guns and knapsacks and everything they had. Our boys picked up some of their vests and shirts out of their knapsacks. There was some nice ones.
    We come up to Baltimore and stayed there a day or two and then took the cars to Washington and then we went to Poolesville and crossed the river and our corps is going down the Shenandoah Valley, but me and two or three of the other boys happened to be behind, and we was all that hadn't crossed must fall back to Fort Reno and we was glad of it.
    We got back this morning and I came over to Mrs. Feaks and I am here now. The 19 Corps was ordered back here too and we expect the Sixth Corps will be here soon. There was a woman gave me a nice straw [hat] in Baltimore and a good dinner and a new kind of a penny to remember her by. We got lots of lemonade and stuff to eat in Washington. I meant to have write to you before but some way I hadn't the chance to get it to the office. I knowed you would be uneasy when you heard of this battle. We ain't none of us had any letters lately. We ain't had no chance to get the mail to us but I hope we shall before long. I don't know how long our regiment will stay here when they get here but I don't think they will stay long. I think they will go right to the front again but I hope not.
    When we was to Baltimore, me and Bill Burt got eight blankets and we put them in a box and I directed to your pa. I might just as well sent twenty of them if I had a- known that we would

have stayed there as long as we did. The boys had all they was a-mind to carry. All they had to do was to go into the cars and get them.

From your ever true and affectionate husband C McDowell Goodbye for this time.

Although the Union lost heavily in the Battle of Monocacy (2000 men while the Confederates lost 700), stalling Early's raid bought Washington time to adequately defend itself. As a result, Washington was saved.

The rest of the war would be taken to the South.

The young Mrs. Seward remembers learning about the Battle of Monocacy: "On Sunday morning, July 10th, I was staying at my mother's, when about noon, my sister, Mrs. Pomeroy, and her husband came in. Mr. Pomeroy said, 'There was a battle at Monocacy, Maryland, yesterday.'

"I said, 'Will could not have been in that, as he is down in front of Petersburgh, VA.'

"No,' he replied, the 9th Artillery were in the battle.' I looked at him startled, and he then said, 'It is reported that Will is wounded and taken prisoner.'

"At the request of Mr. Pomeroy, the telegraph office was kept open all that day and the following night, and he and Mr. Bostwick took turns in watching the news that passed over the wires. The telegraph and railroad lines between Baltimore and Washington had been cut off by rebels so the news from there was received through couriers to Annapolis. I went to Mrs. Seward, and we concluded to pack our trunks, and be ready to start for Washington as soon as railroad communications were reopened. All night my two brothers-in-law waited and watched until 2 o'clock, when a dispatch came, saying 'Colonel Seward wounded, but not a prisoner.' Major Taft was shot and lost his leg. Surgeon Chamberlain stayed with him, and both were taken prisoners.

"My husband's horse was shot under him, and falling upon him, broke his ankle. He also received a slight wound in the arm. He escaped being taken prisoner from the fact of his having on a private's uniform, as he had lost his own at the Battle of Cold Harbor. After the rebel line had passed over him, he crawled on the ground to a piece of woods, where he found a mule [It happened to be one of his own pack mules left behind by his orderly], which, with the help of a straggler, he mounted, using his red silk pocket handkerchief for a bit and bridle, and rode about fifteen miles during the night to Ellicott's Mills, and overtook his retreating regiment...

"[Seward's] horse lay on the field with a wound in the neck, apparently dead, but shortly after recovering from the shock, followed the troops, overtook the retreating orderly... who seeing the blood streaming from the poor animal's neck, staunched its flow with the contents of his tobacco pouch, and took him to Washington, where his wound was properly cared for. He continued in my husband's service.

In September, my husband received a commission as brigadier general, conferred upon him for his service at the battle of Monocacy" (Roe 406-408).

Seward's torn uniform from the Battle of Monocacy is currently displayed at The Seward House in Auburn.

Lincoln congratulates troops:
"President Lincoln drove out to our camp to congratulate the troops on their stubborn resistance at Monocacy. His carriage stopped in the midst of our regiment and the boys gathered about him in great crowds. A tall stripling of a lad of Company D crowded his way to the carriage, and, handing the president the eagle-plate from his cartridge-box straps, with a Confederate bullet sticking fast in its centre, said, 'See, Mr. Lincoln, this saved my life at Monocacy; the force of the bullet knocked me down.' The president took the relic in his hand, looked it over carefully, and after commenting on the fortunate escape of the soldier with the man who sat beside him - a member of the Cabinet, probably Seward - he handed it back to the soldier, saying, 'Young man, keep that for your children and grand-children, for future generations will prize that as the greatest heirloom you could possibly leave them.'" (Roe 136)

To Nancy from Charles (written on Nancy's July the 5 letter):

[Mount Pleasant Hospital]   *July the 20-1864*
Dearest Wife,
Some of us is pretty well tired of marchin. We had a chance to go to the hospital and I thought I would go and have a rest. I have just come here and had a bath and I feel first-rate.

You may send me a postage stamp when you send a letter. Norman York [their good friend and neighbor from home] and a good many I spose is taken prisoners. I will write more to you next time. Direct your letter to Mount Pleaseant hospital Washington D.C.

To Charles from Nancy:

Dearest Husband,   July the 23 1864
    I guess you was glad enough to get to Miss Feaks. I wish that I would have been there. I wish that you could stay there now all winter. I bet you would see me there. I would like no better fun than to come out there and stay this winter.
    I hear that Hank Ellis was killed. His folks feels purty bad about him.
    If you are at Fort Reno when you get this, tell Miss Feaks that I am well and would like to hear from her and would like to see her very much. I would like to know if Miss Snider was there yet. You can't begin to think what the folk told about me when I come home. They [say] that I got rid of a young one and they said that I had the small pox and say that I had the bad disorder. And I think it is ridiculous to be talked about in that way but I can't help myself and so I will hafto stand it. But if all of them behaves themselves as well as I did, they will do well enough I think. As near as I can hear it [is] Miss Browers' talk. If I can find out that it was her, I will tell her what I think about it because I think that I am as good as she is.
    I sent you some camphor gum in the newspapers and I sent you a dollar in a letter.
    From your ever true and affectionate wife Nancy McDowell

To Nancy from Charles:

(Camp Distribution)   July the 27 1864
Dearest Wife,
    I am now at Camp Distribution. I expect to join my company in a day or two.
    Our regiment is going back in the fortifications again. They went in a Sund[ay] but eight companies was ordered yesterday for two or three days to go on that raid towards Harpers Ferry.
    Direct when you write to the regiment same as you always did, only I wouldn't put on the corps and division. Write as soon as you can.
    From your ever true and affectionate husband C McDowell

To Charles from Nancy:

Dearest Husband,   *July 27 1864*

    I am very sorry to hear that you was so near tired out but I feel very thankful to think that you can rest now. I wish that you could stay there [till] your time [is] out. I would stay as long as I could if I was you. We just got a letter from Dave. He is at Fort Reno. When he was coming through Washington he saw Eb. He was just going home.

    I feel very thankful to think that you did not get taking prisoner. Lib [York] must feel bad about Norman [York]. Bill Anson's funeral sermon is to be preached next Sunday to York settlement. They say that Bill Wager wrote home that he was shot dead. They think that Bill Burt and Levy Dunbar and Levy Alan is taken prisoners. They can't hear from them. I heard that Major Taft had sent to his wife if she wanted to see him alive [she] was to come as quick as she could. She started day before yesterday.

    We expect Stephen Wager home this month. Miss Cary hasn't heard from Mr. Cary yet. She think that he is dead [he in fact died in July 10th in a hospital in White House, Virginia].

    They think they won't draft around here. I hope that they will, them old copperheads [Northerners who sympathize with the South]. I want them to go.

To Charles from Nancy:

Dear Husband,   *August 5 1864*

    I haven't heard from you in some time. I am afraid that you are sick but I hope not.

    Pa went and got them blankets yesterday. I think they are splendid blankets. The box cost 2 Dollars and 6 shillings. I think they come real cheap. Miss Burt was here last night and paid for hern.

    We expect Stephen Wager home every day now

    Uncle Henry Dunbar is very sick. They don't think that he will live. He has got the cholera. He was taken last Sunday after he got home from Bill Anson funeral. Hank Juel has got a daughter. Samuel Thompson is a prisoner now.

It has rained all day. It is the first rainy day we have had this summer. It seems good to have it rain. Miss Baker's boy that was in company H is wounded.

From your ever true and affectionate wife to her husband.

To Charles from Nancy:

Dearest Husband,   Sunday August the 8 1864

I am well at present but very lonesome. But I can put up with that and hope that these few lines will find you well and in good health.

We got a letter from Dave last Friday. He said that you was well and you was to Fort Stevens [where Early's troops attacked Washington after the Battle of Monocacy] but I don't know where that is. Dave said that they was afraid that the rebs would attack them again. If they do I hope that our folks will be enough for them. If they do has another fight I want you to write as soon as you can for I shall think that you have got hurt.

The draft makes the men fly around I tell you. Frank Weks is all most scairt to death. I hope that he will haft to go. This time it takes the rich as well as the poor. They have been to Canada to hire substitutes but they doesn't go there any more. They put them to jail and pay a large fine. I am glad of that. Davoo from Lyons they say is in jail too.

Hank Perkins lost his little girl. Charly Knox wife looks like a ghost. They say that she lost her baby. She was four months gone. It was a boy.

Lib Burt is a third larger than she was when you saw her. She is so fat and tall to what she was.

I get a [letter] from Will some time ago and I sent it to you but I don't [know] whether you will get it or not. I answered it as soon as I got it. It was before the raid that I got it.

From you ever true and affectionate wife Nancy McDowell

I close hoping to hear from you soon so goodbye for this time

To Nancy from Charles (written on Nancy's August 5th and July the 23rd letter):
[Fort Reno] *August the 10-1864*
Dear Wife,
    I received your letter last night and I was glad to hear that you are well. I am well at present. I never felt better. I am getting as fat as a pig.
    I have been to Fort Stevens a spell but I am now at Fort Reno. There is four of our companies here now and we expect the others here in a day or two. We live first-rate here. --- We have green corn, potato---a tomatoes and everything.
    Me and Dave went to the city yesterday. We went to the Christian Commission and they gave us lots of stuff. They gave us shoes and summer coats, shirts, drawers toure[?] and handkerchiefs and other little notions. We begin to think now that we will stay around the defenses for a spell.
    I don't think Billy Anson is dead. I think he is wounded and at Frederick, but Levi Dunbar, N York, Lem Rigs, Eben Newburyt, Lu Mun, and four or five more of the new recruits it taken prisoners. There is a good many of the boys wounded but not many of them killed. We had a hard time there [at the Battle of Monocacy] but I am thankful that I got out alive. I [had] some pretty close calls. A piece of shell come and knocked the lock off on my gun and broke the stock pretty well. We can fight the rebs here with a good stomach, but when we heft to go to Petersburg where the sand is up to a fellows eyes, it don't go so well.
    You wanted to know if there was any soldiers to Fort Simmons. There is but they are Hundred Days men. Their time is most out.
    From your husband C McDowell to his wife

To Charles from Nancy:

Dearest Husband, *August [1864]*
    The blackberries is all gone and now I am drying apples now. Lew Williams has got home. He is getting better.
    We are thrashing today and it rains some.
    The Doctor Harry is going to war. Ben Tindall is going for a substitute. He gets a thousand dollars but I am sorry to see him

go for then they won't draft and t___ won't any of the old copperheads hafto go. I would like to see them go first-rate.

The weather is as much too wet as it was to dry.

From you ever true and affectionate wife Nancy McDowell

To Charles from Nancy:

Dearest Husband, *August the 12 [1864]*
I haven't heard from you in some time. I am afraid that you are hurt in the last battle. They say that they have had a hard one. Some says that our folks whipped the rebs and some says that the rebs whipped [us]. So you can't tell anything about it.

The blackberries is very thick this fall. We pick them to sell yesterday. I picked ninety cents worth and today I think I have got more than I had yesterday. Jany Rork [?] takes them to Geneva and Watterloo and sells them.

They don't hear anything from the boys that they took prisoners. Miss Cary hasn't heard from Joe Cary yet. She feels purty bad about him. I feel very thankful to think that yous on your last year now. I think that if your life can be sparred one year more that you can come home once more.

Uncle Henry Dunbar is some better now. His liver has growed so that it shows from the outside. Been and Al Seager will hafto dance in the hog troth for their brother younger then they are is married. He looks about like Mat. A green boy. He married EllSa Hart.

The draft makes the men look wild. I guess it will make some of the old copperheads come in the run for Canada.

From you ever true wife Nancy McDowell

To Nancy from Charles (written on Nancy's August 12th letter):

[Perhaps Fort Reno] *August the 17-1864*
Dearest Wife,
I am on picket now sitting on a big rock.

It has been raining hard. We have had two showers but it has cleared off now and I have just got my dinner. I had tea, meat, sugar and bread and pears and apples and tomatoes, but my bread is pretty wet. I have got it out in the sun now to dry.

You say the blackberries is thick out there now. I wish I was there to go with [you] to pick blackberry. I'll bet you I would have as many as I could eat for once. I think you picked a good many in a day. You mustn't work too hard [in] this hot weather for it might make you sick.

You say you haven't heard from me in some time. I have written two or three letters lately to you, but before that, I was around so all over I could not write, but I will write oftener now. You say that Mrs. Cary hasn't heard from her man in a good while. I heard a spell ago that he was at Philadelphia wounded and he was doing well but I will inquire of the boys and let you know how he is.

You say this is the last year. Yes and I ain't much sorry, but I am thankful that I have got through so far as well as I have. Time passes fast with us now. The year will soon pass off.

I was to Mrs. Feaks yesterday. She ain't very well. I told her that you sent your compliments to her. She told me to tell you you must come yourself and bring them in both hands. She says she wants you to come and take care of her.

From your ever true and affectionate husband C McDowell

To Charles from Nancy:

Dearest Husband,   *August the 18 1864*

I was very glad to hear that you have something good to eat. We haven't had no green corn nor tomatoes and our potatoes is very small. It was so dry that they could not grow.

I am picking some berries and drying some apples and ma is doing about the same. Pa is cutting oats and so is Mat. My she don't do much.

The first draft went off yesterday they say. But we don't [know] who it drafted yet.

I feel very sorry for John Vannatwert. He must feel very bad. I did not think that she [his wife] would live long. I don't hardly think that Art Scott is alive for he was almost gone with the consumption when he got his discharge.

I haven't heard anything about the trunk. I guess it will hafto go. I druther lost my trunk than come out as Miss Vannatwerp did, for the doctor sayed that if I had stayed four weeks longer, there would not have been any help for my bowels. Would have been ulcered clear through, but now I am as well as I ever was, I think. But I thought one spell that I never would get well. I don't think my doctor's bill will be more than three dollars. You wanted me to keep the paper of the killed and wounded. I have sent them to you.

     I have picked four dollars worth of berries and sold them. Mary Dunbar has applied for Bill Anson's bounty. I think it is most too bad for her to get it if he is not dead. I should think that the officers would know. Harry Perkins has enlisted. Jim Sofa is riding around here as big as cufy [?]. I would like to know if he got his discharge. He has took off his soldiers.

To Nancy from Charles:

(Tennallytown)   August the 22-1864
Dearest Wife,
     I wrote a letter to you when I was on picket. When I came off our company had moved to Fort Summer, the other side of Fort Mansfield and that afternoon me and Dave was detailed to go to Tennallytown to do provost duty. There was 23 went out of our regiment. Only me and Dave went out of our company.
     We have got some wall tents and we are living pretty comfortable. We haft to go to Washington pretty often with prisoners but our duty is light. I don't know how long we will be kept here. We are all a-going to draw new clothes today and I spose we shall heft to keep dreadful nice. One thing, we ain't no fatigue duty to do. I ain't done anything since I left Petersburg. I never see such easy times. I hope that they will continue until my time is out.
     I am down to Mrs. Feaks pretty often lately. I guess the draft begins to draw pretty close on them out there now. Captain has resigned and gone home. The poor cowardly whelp. Our regiment has been scattered all over the world but they will [be] coming in now pretty fast. The most of them is at Fort Simmons and Mansfield and Fort Gains.
     From your ever true and affectionate husband C McDowell

To Nancy from Charles:

[Tennallytown]   *August the 31-1864*
Dearest Wife,

    I never was in better health. I can eat my loaf of bread at two meals easy and look for more but I am getting as fat as a pig.

    We are at Tenallytown yet doing provost duty. I don't know how long we will stay here but I hope all winter. We have nothing to do only take prisoners to Washington and parole through the country for straggling soldiers and find out who lets liquor to them and we go through orchards and all over where we are a-mind to. We get all the apples and peaches we are a-mind to eat. I wish you could be here and help eat some of the peaches that I had the other day. They was splendid and I wish I was out there to help you pick blackberries and I wish a good many things but it don't seem to do me much good, but I can't grumble when I have as easy times as I have now.

    For a few days back all I heft to do is to take the lieutenant's horse backward and forwards to the stable and bring a little water but I don't [know] how long it will last but I hope it will last till my time is out. I think you have done real well picking blackberries.

    There is great times here about the boys re-enlisting. I do believe there is more than half of our regiment that will enlist. It is pretty tempting. Such high bounties and a thirty-day furlough.

    We have drawed us all new clothes. We heft to keep neat here. We heft to wear the white gloves.

    What do they heft to pay for hands to work around there now?

    From you ever true and affectionate husband C McDowell

Colonel Seward was promoted to brigadier general and was headquartered in Martinsburg. "August 23rd Colonel Seward comes out from Washington and is anxious to have the regiment united...'Apparently the colonel would rather have us together in h__l than separated in Heaven.' Whatever his wishes he was never to see the men together again" (Roe 159).

Sept 2, 1864 - Sherman's army captures Atlanta. A great victory for Lincoln and the North.

To Nancy from Charles:

[Tenallytown]   *Sept the 4-1864*
Dearest Wife,
    We are at Tennallytown yet. We are having splendid nice weather her[e] now.
    There is quite an excitement here about re-enlisting. I bet you two thirds of the army will enlist. Grant's army is rather getting the start of the rebs now but they ain't whipped yet. They are tough fellows. I soon found that out when we went to the front.
    You wouldn't hardly know me now. I hadn't shaved since we started for the front till today and my mustache got so long I couldn't eat molasses very well and I cut it off and most all the rest of my whiskers. The boys don't hardly know me.
    John Perkins is a prisoner. Fred Stell is killed. We can't hear much about the prisoners.
    From your ever true and affectionate husband, C McDowell

To Charles from Nancy:

Dearest Husband,   September 4 1864
    I have just got the letter that you wrote the fourth of July. I don't think purty much of that girl being so clever. High Thompson, he found some clever ones out there. The folks says that he has got the clap [gonorrhea] so that they can't go in the house because he smells so bad, and they don't think that he will live long. They thought he was dead one day. The doctor had been fixing him.
    The cannons roared all night last night. They don't know what it was for but they think is some good news. They say that we have taking Mobile and they think that Petersburg will be ourn in a week's time. I hope it is all true but I am afraid it is almost too good to be true. They say that Old Abe says the war will end in three months.
    You say that you go and see Miss Feaks purty often. I wish I was there so I could go with you. I hope that you can stay to Tennallytown till your time is out. It seams almost like an age. A whole year before you can come home but I am glad every time when night comes. I think one more day has past and gone and

your time is so much nearer out but it will pass off after a while. It can't last always.

Hank Jule is drafted. I don't know whether he will go or not. They have filled up Huron's call. They give them fifteen hundred apiece, but Sodus, they will hafto come to a draft for there has so many run too.

The paper states that they are paying all the armies off now but I though[t] your being to Tennallytown your wouldn't get your pay. I would like to know if your have heard anything from Cary or not. She hasn't heard from him since he was...

From your ever true and affectionate wife Nancy McDowell

To Charles from Nancy:

Dearest Husband, September the 11 1864

You spoke about the regiment enlisting again. I hope that you won't be so foolish to enlist again. I had drather go with half enough to eat than have you enlist again. The big bounty I would[n't] look at it. I had drather have my freedom than all the money.

The men get from two dollars to twenty sh_____ pr day and thirty dollars pr month. Any body can earn a living, and if you get hurt, I can work ____ get us a living. I would work night and bet you should have enough to eat. I wouldn't have you enlist again for two thousands dollars if I could have my way about it. You said that your captain resigned and had gone home. Who is your captain now?

I sent you some camphor gum I would like to know if you got it. I would like to have your likeness since you shaved. I think I would know it.

Am here all alone today. All the rest has gone to meeting. I wish you was here with me. This makes me think of my dream last night. I thought I was out there with you and we was up to Miss Feaks and we had a good visit and we was carrying on like everything and I laugh so loud that it woke me up. I have thought about it all [?] morning

Dave wrote home to know what Pa and Ma thought about his enlisting. I think he is foolish. He said he wouldn't enlist for all of Verginey. I think he turns his tune but [?] him enlist. Don't you?

    I don't suppose that [you] hafto stand guard nights now.
From your ever true affectionate wife

To Nancy from Charles:

[Probably Tennallytown]   Sept the 12 - 1864
Dearest Wife

    We have had a considerable of rain lately and it is pretty cool weather here now. They say Hammond and his wife had a quarrel and he has enlisted.

    I got the letter that had the dollar in I guess I won't send it back for I have got it most all spent for apple dumplings and milk. There is peddlers here all the while with them and you know how I like dumplings. I wish you was here now to make another such a batch as we had last winter. I think I could manage some of them. They are ten cts apiece. Mrs. Hoxie has 25 cts apiece for pies now, 75 cts a meal.

    That fellow that [you] spoke about [the one with the "clap"] is pretty bad off. You talk as though you thought I might get in that way. But Nat you needn't be uneasy about that and I don't think I am quite as soft in the head as to go in such speculations as that and I don't think that you would think that I would do any such a thing. Anyway if you do, you are greatly mistaken.

    What does the folks think about election out there? Here the most of them thinks Old Abe will get it again and I think so and I think the war will be settled under him as quickly as any body else. The most the rebs is waiting now is election. I think they will come to some settlement after election. They would like to have McClellan in if they could.

    I was to Mrs. Feaks today. She is well. I left a nice little there that I found. She wants me to give it to her but I don't know whether to give it to her or send it home.

    You said you was pretty lonesome. I dare say you be Nat but you must keep up good courage. The time will soon run round when I can be at home again. Sometimes I feel very lonesome, but when I think of the time and how fast it is passing, I get over it again. If I can get through the remainder of my time as well as I have the fore part I shall feel very thankful, although I have had some pretty close calls.

I think I told you that at Monocacy a piece of shell or a ball broke my gun and Carpenter told me to throw it away and pick up another and I picked up a nice rifle. You could have picked up a gun there any place. I was afraid I would get over heated that day for I was one of the last off of the field and I was awful warm when I came off, and then we had to take a double quick once and a while to keep out of their batteries, and I was most choked for a drink, but I doesn't drink much. I was so warm and another thing, we hadn't any too much time to get it.

I ain't doing much of anything but I get just as much pay as though I had worked hard. I am afraid I have got in a bad place to learn how to work but I guess I can learn how when I get home again

From your ever true and affectionate husband c. McDowell

I hadn't but just my letter finished when we had orders to move. We are in Washington now waiting for cars to take us to Harpers Ferry. We have got orders to fall in now.

Chapter Eleven

Sheridan's Shenandoah Valley campaign
The Battles of Opequon (or Winchester), Fisher's Hill and Cedar Creek

To Nancy from Charles:

(Near Berrysville - 22 miles from Harpers Ferry)   Sept the 18-64
Dearest Wife,

We lay in front of the enemy but there is no fighting on either side, and I guess there won't be any very quick without they attack us. All we want is to keep them here at present.

We are encamped in the woods. It's a nice place but we don't know how long we will stay here. We are about 22 miles from

Harpers Ferry near Berryville. That letter that had that dollar in ain't here nor them papers. I guess that is lost. I got your letter dated the 11 when we was at Washington. Carpenter is acting as captain now.

You say you was alone. I know you was lonesome but you must keep up good courage. I feel in hopes that I shall soon be with you. Now you had quite a dream. I would have been glad if it had been true. You said you didn't want me to enlist. You needn't be scart. I don't [I] think shall if you didn't want me to. I shouldn't anyway for all the money they can stack up.

From your ever true and affectionate husband C. McDowell

Charles was now under the command of Sheridan. "Grant's instructions were grimly specific. He wanted the rich farmlands of the [Shenandoah] Valley despoiled so thoroughly that the place could no longer support a Confederate army...that a crow flying across over the Valley would have to carry its own rations. This work Sheridan set out to do...

"On the nineteenth...[Sheridan] fought Early near the town of Winchester, Virginia. The battle began before half of Sheridan's army had reached the scene, and the morning hours saw a Union repulse, but by mid afternoon Sheridan had all of his men in hand, and Early was badly beaten and compelled to retreat. Sheridan pursued, winning another battle at Fisher's Hill three days later, and Early continued on up the Valley while Sheridan's men got on the job of devastation Grant had ordered." (Catton, 244-246)

To Charles from Nancy:

Dearest Husband,   *Sept the 22 1864*

I am very sorry to think that you are on a march again. I was in hopes that you could stay to Tennallytown the rest of your time, but one will hafto put up with the hardships of war. But I am very thankful that you are on the last year. If your life is spared, you won't hafto stay away always. I will be so glad when your time is out and you come home once more.

Levy Allen is dead. They expect him home last night or this morning. He died with the chronic diarrhea. His brother went to see him and he was a- coming home and he died the same day that they was a- going to start for home. That is the first one that has died with disease in a good while and I hope it may be the last one.

We are all [busy] drying apples.

From your ever true and affectionate wife to her dearest husband.

The Battle of Winchester

To Nancy from Charles:

Dearest Wife,   *Sept the 23-64*

We have had some pretty hard fighting with the rebs. We commenced fighting on the 19 and we fight all day and we whipped them awfully. We drove them through Winchester. They was a regular panic stricken. Their own artillery and wagons run over some of their own men. They left three thousand of their wounded in Winchester. We are still in pursuit. We are have taken lots of prisoners and a good many pieces of artillery. Old Ewels[?] is gave up. We lost a considerable many men in our regiment but not many in our company. Ander Rineheart was shot dead. John Faloon they don't think will live and 2 or three more wounded but some of the other companies lost pretty heavy. I tell you there is dreadful work through here now but we are taking the rebs on every side. Some of our boys is standing guard over a reb major. They have got him a black smith shop.

I was talking with some of the Co. C men. They say Cary is at some hospital. They heard from him not long ago. He is doing well. [He died back on July 10th].

From your ever true and affectionate husband C McDowell

Joe Sage is badly wounded but I am thankful that I am safe and well. You must excuse all mistakes for I expect to pack and travel every minute.

"How it struck the Confederates themselves appears in the following wail taken from the diary of a wounded prisoner, confined in Winchester: 'I never saw troops in such confusion before. Night found Sheridan's hosts in full and exultant possession of much-abused, beloved

Winchester. The hotel hospital was pretty full of desperately wounded and dying Confederates. The entire building was shrouded in darkness during shrieks, prayers and oaths of the wretched sufferers, combined with my own severe pain, banished all thoughts of rest...Our scattered troops, closely followed by the large array of pursuers, retreated rapidly and in disorder through the city. It was a sad, humiliating sight.'" (Roe 154)

To Stephen Wager from cousin Almira (Nancy's sister) in an envelope addressed to him at General hospital Ward Philadelphia:

Dear Cousin   *Sept the 25, 1864*
Stephen I take pen in hand to write you a few lines to let you now we are well. We haint heard from you in quite a long time and I thought I would write you a few lines. Pa sent you a letter a spell ago and we was waiting for an answer or for you to come home. You said you was comin' this month if nothing happened. I was afraid that you was sick or some thing and so I thought I would write. I hope you will come and fetch the answer to this and if you can't, write as soon as you can. We all want to see you and I hope we shall before long. Till then, goodbye
From you cousin Almira

To Charles from Nancy:

Dearest Husband,   *September the 25 [1864*
Levy Alan's funeral was today but they did not show him. They had kep him so long.
You said that you was in a nice place. I hope that you can stay there and I hope that you won't hafto fight. I dread that when we hear that there going to be a battle or there has been a battle for I think that you are killed or wounded. It is awful to think of how many poor men loses their lives for their country. I will be so glad when this cruel war is over so all the men can return to their friends.
Samuel Thompson time is out and he is in the Liby prison. That is terrible. I [think] they ought to let him come home.
Dave Courtright has been here. He is as fat as a pig. Alf Courtright he is wounded through his shoulder. Mr. Browers has got back again. They live in Pa's house.

I got me a new pair of shoes the other day with the rest of my berry money. They cost three dollars and a half. Do you think I was extravagant? I am a- going to keep them till you come. If you ever do. I thought I would get them and then I would have a nice pair seeing that I earnt the money myself.

Our peaches is all soft. I wish you was here to help eat some of them. We are drying them as fast as we can.

From your ever true and affectionate wife to her dearest husband.

From Nancy to Charly.

I am sorry that letter that had the dollar in [it] is lost and the papers

To Charles from Nancy:

Dearest Husband,   Oct the 1 [1864]

The paper stated of hard [fighting] the 28 [?] but I hope the Lord has spared your life.

Poor Miss Rhinehart. It will make her almost crazy. Her health is very poor. I hope that I may never get any such news but I expect it every day when there is fighting but I hope for the best.

Stephen Wager has got home. Poor fellow. He has lost his right arm. It is just about a finger long from the shoulder joint. He looks bad enough. He looks as if he had been hewed down. Some says they just as lived [?] a been killed as come off as he did but I would drather been in his place. But if it had been his leg it would have been better, I think, for now you hafto cut all his victuals up on his plate. He can't help himself at all.

Charly Case was here the other day. He has lost part of his left hand and Spencer Case has enlisted for this big bounty. Emma Frolle's [?] man is drafted and so is Alonso Tindall. Ed Camp and lots of other ones, they are in the mallcy [?]. It seems like a sham draft as if it wouldn't mount to anything.

They had another party last night. I think it is most too bad to dance in such a times as it is now.

They say that everything is coming down. Butter has been fifty cents but now they won't hardly buy it and give anything much for it. You said that you had looked for letters from me. I write two every week and I don't see why you don't [get] them. Miss

Carry thinks that Joe Carry is dead and she is trying to sell his place. The folks says that Joe Carry has got two women, but it may be all false. They talk so much now [a] day. They will lie to make their story sound good, but I don't [know] anything about it.

I am very thankful to think that you got through that battle. I do feel sorrow for folks that loses their friends in the war.

I can't think of any more at present only write soon and give me all the news. I would like to get one every day--it is all the comfort that I take, reading your letters.

From your every true and affectionate wife Nancy McDowell to her dearest husband Charles McDowell.

To Nancy from Charles:

(Harrisonburg) Oct the 2-1864
Dearest Wife,

I now take the opportunity to answer your kind and welcome letter which was dated the 17. We are about one hundred miles from Harpers Ferry. It was quite a march. The boys some of them had pretty sore feet. We lay now at Harrisonburg.

We was 8 mls below Harrisonburg towards Stanton but we marched back. They have burnt mills and barns and everything else that would aid the rebels. We sent the rebs whirling through this valley. I don't think they will want to come back. They say we have taken ten thousand prisoners. We fetch in some from these mountains most every day. We chased them so close they put in there to hide. We took 27 pieces of Artillery at Winchester and Fishers Gap that I see and how many more I don't know but we destroyed their army here. John Faloon is dead. Levi Allen is dead. He died with sickness.

You say I didn't tell you what I gave Mrs. Feak. It was a little rifle. The whole regiment is here now. They say the paymaster is here to pay us off. Tell your pa that I should like to be there to help him log but I have got about all the logging I can tend to at present but maybe he can save some till next fall then I will help him. We don't get mail here very often. It only comes when the train comes. I haven't much time to write any more as the train is just ready to start out. We have lived on pancakes for a few days back and fresh pork and potatoes and cabbage and molasses. One

day feast and next a famine. We make pancakes out of wheat flour that we captured. They ain't very light but they taste very well.
   From your ever true and affectionate husband C. McDowell
   What percent can you get on money there now?

Cooking Pancakes. Courtesy of <u>Hard Tack and Coffee</u>

In regards to the vast devastation of the fertile Shenandoah Valley, Bruce Catton writes: "Few campaigns in the war aroused more bitterness than this one. The Union troopers carried out their orders with a heavy hand, and as they did so they were plagued by the attacks of bands of Confederate guerrillas--irregular fighters who were of small account in a pitched battle, but who raided outposts, burned Yankee wagon trains, shot sentries and couriers, and compelled Sheridan to use a sizable percentage of his force for simple guard duty. The Federal soldiers considered the guerrillas no better than highwaymen, and when they captured any of them they usually hanged them. The guerrillas hanged Yankees in return, naturally enough; and from all of this there was a deep scar, burned into the American memory, as the romanticized 'war between brothers' took on an ugly phase.

"Guerrilla warfare tended to get out of hand. Most bands were semi-independent, and in some areas they did the Confederacy harm by draining able-bodied men away from the regular fighting forces and by stimulating the Federals to vicious reprisals. Best of guerrilla leaders was Colonel John S. Mosby, who harassed Sheridan's supply lines so effectively that substantial numbers of Sheridan's troops had to be kept on duty patrolling roads back of the front..." (Catton, 245 & 246)

Charles himself would one day come face to face with Mosby's infamous men.

To Charles from Nancy:

Dearest Husband,   *Oct the 6 1864*
    I hear that Levy Dunbar has got back to his regiment and he says that John Perkins is dead. Lew Williams is most well and he is a hurry to get back to his company. They say he is captain of the company. I should thought Carpenter would have been captain. I saw C Redgraves the...He don't look so well as he did before he had the small pox.
    I went to see Jane Button the other day. She and her sister is most dead with the consumption. They can't do nothing. They are nothing but skin and bones. They are so poor the doctor Hary says they can't either of them live. They was both great big fat girls about a year ago. Their mother feels awful bad about them. Old Mr. Perkins is so low that he don't know nothing. July [Julle?] Cimplen's man wrote home that Joe Carry was on his way home and she thinks he is waiting for his discharge. We heard the other day that the rebs had left Richmond and our folks had it but you can't tell anything about it.
    They have heard from Norman York [their good friend taken prisoner at the Battle of Monocacy]. He writes to George York. He don't write to Lib [his wife]. She is real put out about it to think he wouldn't write to her. I should thought he would have written to her for all writing to his brother and I don't blame her. She says when she writes to him again he will know it.
    From your ever true and affectionate wife to her dearest husband.

To Nancy from Charles:

[Cedar Creek]   *Oct the 16-1864*
Dearest Wife,
    We have had some pretty hard marching again. We got started the other morning. They said we was a- going to Petersburg. We got started and marched about 18 miles and the order was countermand and we turned round and encamp. All night they said Grant had captured Petersburg. Well we started in the morning and marched to Middletown near Fisher's Gap. The Johnnies [Confederate soldiers] got in there again. They had a

fight with the 19 corps but they heard the Sixth was a- coming and I think they have put out. If they ain't we shall have some more fighting to do but I hope that they will leave. I don't think they will find much to eat in the Valley. We have cleaned it out pretty well. We have burnt most everything we came to.

You said you heard that Levi Dunbar was back to the regiment. He ain't been here nor ain't been paroled yet as we know. We heard that Levi Riggs and Hiram Man was paroled but we don't know it for certain. William Burt hasn't gone home for I saw him about 20 minutes ago. We have got a lot of new recruits come here today for our regiment. 25 for our company.

Write soon, for as you say, the most of my comfort is in reading your letters, but the time is not far distant when I hope when we can talk together without writing. I tell you, Nat, won't I be glad when that time comes?

From your ever true and affectionate husband C McDowell

Three days later, on Oct the 19th, the Battle of Cedar Creek was fought. "The middle of October found Sheridan's army encamped near Cedar Creek, twenty miles south of Winchester. Early was not far away but he had been beaten twice and it seemed unlikely that he retained any aggressive intentions, and Sheridan left the army briefly to visit Washington. At dawn on the morning of October 19, just as Sheridan was preparing to leave Winchester and return to camp, Early launched a sudden attack that took the Union army completely by surprise, broke it, and drove various fragments down the road in a highly disordered retreat. Sheridan met these fragments as he was riding back to camp, hauled them back into formation, got them to the battle front, put them in line with the soldiers who had not run away, and late in the afternoon made a furious counterattack which was overwhelmingly successful. Early was driven off, his army too badly manhandled to be a substantial menace any longer, and it was plain to all men that the Confederacy would never again threaten the North by way of the Shenandoah Valley.

This victory aroused much enthusiasm...Sheridan's conquest was a tonic that checked war weariness and created a new spirit of optimism. No longer could the Democrats make an effective campaign on the argument that the war was a failure...Sherman, Farragut and Sheridan were winning Lincoln's election for him." (Catton, 247 –248).

Some of the losses in the New York Ninth:
"It is due to the memory of Lieutenant Orrin B. Carpenter, Company D, who was killed in the early part of the engagement, to say that

although suffering long from fever, and but just able to walk, and having been repeatedly urged for weeks before to go to the hospital, invariably requested to remain with his company, and when the battle commenced was found in line with his men. He was shot through the heart by a rebel sharpshooter while doing his duty and now fills a patriot's grave. Peace be to his ashes. (Roe 179-180)

An account by Charles L. Shergur: "Here one of our boys, Anthony Riley, was shot and killed; his father was by his side; the blood and brains of his son covered the face and hands of the father. I never saw a more affectin sight than this; the poor old man kneels over the body of the dead son; his tears mingle with his son's blood. O God! What a sight; he can stop but a moment, for the rebels are pressing us; he must leave his dying boy in the hands of the devilish foe; he bends over him, kisses his cheek, and with tearful eyes rushes to the fight, determined on revenge for his son." (Roe 181-182)

To Charles from Almira:

Dear Friend, *Oct the 26 [1864?]*
It is snowing here today, the first. Had a very pleasant Fall but folks are not half through with their work yet. I think you must be having hard times down there but you must keep up good courage and do the best you can. You must do as Eb said he did-- dog the bull [?.]
Charly I wish you would do all the fighting up and [get] it done with. What is the use of being so long about it? I thought by your talk you would have them all killed off by this time. We do not hear anything from Eb yet. I cannot think of much to write but be a good boy and come home to Nancy as soon as you can. Goodbye. Please write as soon as you get this, for we are always glad to hear from you.
My pen is poor, my ink is black, if you can't read it send it back.

To Nancy from Charles:

(Near Cedar Creek) *Nov the 6- 1864*
Dearest Wife
I now take the opportunity to answer your kind and welcome letter and was very glad to hear that you are well. I don't

feel as well as I have done along back, as I catched a pretty heavy cold, but I am getting a good deal better.

We have come from Martinsburg back to our old campground near Cedar Creek. When we was coming back we guarded a train and we was attacked by Mosby's men. We had artillery with us and we gave them a few rounds of that and they fled for the woods. They took a general that was with us. He and his aids was on the lead and they got him, but the rest put spur to their horses and came back safe. We had sixteen paymasters with us coming to pay off the troops. They would have got a good big pile of money if they would have took them. We had two good batteries and a good many men. We had seven hundred wagons in the train we came with.

A train comes in here most every day now. Part of our regiment has gone again to guard a train. One company went, all but five or six[of us], and I stayed with [them] because I didn't feel very well.

Some of our boys that was shot in the last battle is buried right here in our campground. Lieutenant Howard had most all of his head shot off by a shell. He is buried here.

Samuel Lape has got a Dishonorable Discharge from the service. He left on suspicion. They don't know where he is gone. I read it in the paper the other day.

You say Nancy that you feel bad when you hear of a battle. I dare say you do, but Nat you must keep up good courage. It will be only a few months, if I am spared, before I can be with you then I think that we can take comfort.

We expected an attack this morning. We was up and ready at three o'clock in the morning. If I had stayed to Martinsburg a day or two longer I could have got a furlough to went home. There was some of them that went. But if I live till next Fall, then I can come to stay. That will be better than any furlough.

It snowed here a little yesterday. You would laugh to see the way we fix our little tent. We have got a little fireplace right in front. It makes it quite comfortable.

Write as often as you can because that is the most comfort that I take in reading your letters. I have just bought me a overcoat, most new. I gave three dollars for it.

From you ever true and affectionate husband C. McDowell

To Charles from Nancy:

Dearest Husband,   *November the 10 1864*

    Been Seager has got home. He got home the same day that his brother's wife was buried. He didn't know that he was married till he got home, now that she was dead.

    Yesterday there was a man shot himself. He went out a-hunting and hid his gun in some boards, and when he went to get it, he took holt of the muzzle of the gun and went to pull it out. It went off and hit him in the eye.

    The money that you sent, I am a-going to keep it all, but five dollars, and then we will have six hundred and twenty five dollar. And I can take my certificate and draw the five dollars out of the bank that don't draw but five per cent and what you sent home I can keep.

    We don't know who is elected yet but Huron went two hundred and fifty republicans. I want to know who you voted for, or didn't you vote at all?. There was a good many soldiers home to vote. I wished that you could have come home too.

    So goodbye for this time.

    From you ever true and affectionate wife Nancy McDowell

    There is nothing going on here and it is very lonesome.

To Charles from Nancy:

Dearest Husband,   *November the 16 1864*

    I was very glad to hear from you but was very sorry to hear that you was sick. It was almost three weeks since I heard from you. I did not know what was the matter.

    I heard that Robert Traver was dead. Levy Dunbar is at home. He was over here. He looks purty health. Al and Dave Courtright is to home. Alf is stationed to Rochester now. I wish you was there so that I could come and see you. That would be nice. The time would pass of quicker. Samuel Lape is to home, they say come from Canada. I heard from Eb the other...

    It is so very lonesome here. I can't hardly stand it.

    Ike Woodruff's father is dead. He died very sudden. He was sick four days. He had the inflammation in the bowels. He was taken when he was picken up apples. The ground is all covered with snow but there isn't enough for sleighing yet. The folks isn't ready for winter yet. They haven't all got their corn husked yet.

From you ever true and affectionate wife Nancy McDowell

To Charles from Nancy:

Dearest Husband,   *Novem the 25 [1864?]*

I got a letter from you last night and was very glad to hear from you but was sorry to hear that you are so near the rebs for fear you will get hurt.

They had John Perkins' funeral last Sunday. I was there. Hi Nap was there too. There has been lots of soldiers home to election but they have about all of them gone back.

We have got dun drying apples. Ma had a hundred and seven dollars worth of apples. She gave me thirteen dollars of it. I have earned 23 dollars this summer. That is more than every soldier's wife earnt that had a better chance than I had.

The democrats says they got skunked. They didn't get the first democrats in.

Miss Cary thinks that Joseph Cary is dead [he had been for over four months] and she is flying around with the Courtright boys. First one then the other. I think she must think herself in purty business don't you? Do you hear anymore about him? Do you know whether Traver is dead? I heard he was dead. Do you hear from Miss Feaks? I would like to hear from her.

I am glad to hear that you had some fresh pork for you had something to eat then. I think of that every day when I go to eat.

From you every true and affectionate wife Nancy McDowell

To Nancy's father Charles Wager from Nancy's cousin Stephen Wager:

Dear Uncle,   *December 3, 1864*

I was almost three days a-coming out here and then it took the rest part of the day to find the hospital, but after a while, I found it. I came in and reported to the doctor.

He says to me, "Where have you been."

I says to the doctor, "I have been to home."

The doctor says to me, "What made you stay so long?"

I says, "I had business to do."
The doctor says, "What was your business?"
I says to doctor, "I had my county bounty to get."
"Well," he says, " that didn't keep you so long."
"Well," I says, "I thought I might as well be at home for I was no expense to the government, and if I was here, I would be."
"Well," he says to the corporal of the guard, "Put him in the guard house."
So I had to make my home in there that night, and the next day about noon, another doctor sent [for] the corporal and [he] told me that the doctor wanted to see me and [I] went in and he said to me, "Who gave you permission to go home?"
I told him, "Nobody." Then I told him I put in twice for a furlough and did not get one.
So he says, "You took one."
I said "Yes."
"Well," he says, "I will let you go this time if you will promise me you won't do it again." I told him I would not. He said I could get a furlough as often as I want one.
I wrote a letter last night to Polly and one to Rhoda. These three I have written with my left hand. You must not expect me too much the first beginen. Give my love to all. So goodbye for this time.

"On the morning of Dec. 3d, the regiment with the brigade marched to Stevenson's Depot beyond Winchester and were shipped by rail on coal and cattle cars to Washington, accommodations supposed to be good enough for soldiers and certainly preferable to marching if unfortunately they had not been lousy as the result of previous occupation...Passed through Washington on the 4th and at noon went on board steamboats for City Point; arriving there at noon on the 5th at 6 P.M. of the same day took the cars for the front south of Petersburg." (Clark, 611)

To Charles from Nancy:

Dearest Husband,   December 4 1864
    Our folks is all gone away and I am here alone and I have been playing on the accordion. I can play four tunes on it and I got tired and so I thought I would write you a few lines.

Levy Dunbar has got the chronic diarrhea, the same as I had it. James Sofa is dead. He died with the chronic diarrhea and the consumption. They have got the small pox at Sodus Center. There has one died with it--the soldier that brought it home. Bill Burt has got so that he can walk around with a crutch. He is trying to get a furlough to come home. He is to Philadelphia.

Pa had the luck to cut the end of his finger off yesterday while he was making wedge to wedge his ax helve on. It bled purty bad. It is his finger next to his little finger. It did not take quite all the nail. It will lay him up so that he can't chop this winter.

Alonso Tindall is a-going to teach this school here this winter. He begins tomorrow. I think sometimes that I had better go. What do you think about it? I hear of quite a number of married ladies is a-going.

Dave and Miss Cary is married, so they say, and Alf has bought the mortgage of the place and he is going to foreclose in the mortgage and the place is to be sold auction the eight[h] day of March. Pa thinks that it will be sold purty cheep. He thinks that we had better buy it if it goes cheep. We could fix it up a little and sell it for quite good deal more than we paid for it. What do you think about it? If you think it isn't best then let it go, but if you [think] it is a good plan then tell how much that he had better bid. I think it is worth four hundred dollars. That is what Cary paid for it. It is advertised in the Lyons paper.

My sheep - I don't want Pa to have them any longer than next fall, for if you live to come home, then we can take care of them ourselves. There would be hay enough to winter them on and more too. But you can do as you are a-mind to about trying to get it.

From your ever true and affectionate wife Nancy McDowell Goodbye for this time.

Chapter Twelve
The Siege at Petersburg

To Nancy from Charles:

(Near Petersburg)   *Dec the 6-1864*
Dearest Wife,
         We are near Petersburg now. They can't stop racing the Six Corps around. They say they expect to have a big fight here and I expect we shall have a hand in. We always do but I hope we will come out all safe.
         Me and Dave and John Rummels sent a bundle by express. You can get it and take it to your house and John's folks will come and get their things. My overcoat has got a hole burnt in the tail. 1 shirts, 2 pair drawers and a blanket are that I took from a Jonney at the Battle of Cedar Creek. My account book is in there.
         Robert Trevor is doing well. I went to see the captain about Cary. He says he don't think he is dead [he had been dead now for almost five months]. He says he hasn't had no notification of it, and if he is dead, he thinks he would know something about it. But he can't tell for certain.
         We expect to move every minute. It's first here, and then there. It's pretty warm here now.

To Charles from Nancy:

Dearest Husband,   *December the 15 1864*
         I am very sorry to hear that you had to move to Petersburg but was very glad to hear that you was well.
         That likeness is just as natural as life I think. Ma says that you are so fat that you can't see out of your eyes, but I like to see you look so, for then I think you must be well. You want me to send you some money. I will send you a dollar this time and then I will send you one the next time for maybe the letter will get lost and then one dollar is enough to lose at once.
         Eb has been here. You said you did not want to hear from him but I will tell you anyway. He had Elvines Jones' likeness with him. She has got to be real good looking. She looks as if she was as

large as I am. Your uncle Hiram said that Eb sent his money to Uncle Dave's girl. I guess he did not send any, for if he had he would have went there, but he didn't go there. He come right through one end of Canada.

You said that it was real warm there. It is cold enough. It is purty good sleighing.

Pa and Mi is going to Lyons with cutter. It is the first sleigh ride this fall.

Lib York [Norman's wife] has been here to see me. She feels so big I can't hardly go her [?]. She stayed today and tonight but I don't know whether I will return the visit or not. I don't [like] such big folks.

They say that Miss Cary went to Lyons to get Cary's bounty and her pension and she wouldn't take her oath that she was ever married to Cary nor that her yo[ung]one was Cary's so I don't believe she ever was married to Cary. I think she is tough customer.

From you true and affectionate wife Nancy McDowell

To Nancy from Charles:

Camp before Petersburg   Dec the 19-1864
Dearest Wife,

I now take the opportunity to answer your kind and welcome letter and was glad to hear that you are well but am sorry to hear of your pa cutting his finger. He had aughta to have been a little more carefuller handling edged tools. But I find accidents will happen there as well as here. But I hope to hear of it soon getting well.

We have had one pretty hard [jaunt] since we come here but the rest of the time we have took it pretty easy. A few days ago we was marched near the South Side railroad about ten miles from Petersburg to protect the Jonnies from flanking our folks while they tore up the railroad. They tore up 20 miles of road and fell back the night we went down. It was awful cold and it snowed and rained all night and we had to lay in it or set up just as we had a-mind to. That was rather rough but we have come out all right. One fellow catched such a cold that he died yesterday - a new recruit on that raid.

I came acrost a cousin of mine. His name is Sebern. He is from Simcoe C. West. He listed June. He is in the Second Corps. He said he tried to get in this regiment but he couldn't do it. He is sick of it aready. I saw Harvey Perkins yesterday. He is pretty sick of it. He says he ain't been very well lately. I haven't written to Mrs. Feak yet.

You say[you] think you will go to school this winter. I think it would be a very good plan. But about buying that place of Brawers, I don't hardly [know] what to think about it. I think four hundred dollars is a pretty big price for it. I think three hundred is a pretty big price for it. There only about three acres in it but if we could get it cheap enough it would do. It would do well enough to bid on it.

Have you got that accordion fixed yet? Learn all you can on it. You say you have learnt four tunes. You know you learnt one before I came away. I believe that was Yankee Doodle.

From your affectionate husband C McDowell

Sometime when you get a chance I wish you would get a box of ------pills. You can send them in a newspaper. I may would use them before spring and I can't get them here. I bought me another overcoat. I got one as good as the one I sent home for 75 cts. I have got more money coming to me on clothing than any man in our company. I have got 21 dollars and 45 cts coming on last years clothing.

To Nancy from Charles:

Camp near Petersburg   *Dec the 20-1864*
Dearest Wife,

We are out on picket now next to the rebs. We heft to lay low once and a while when we get to exchanging shots with them. We gone on for three days at a time. We will come off tomorrow morning.

You said Nat that you felt worried for fear that I didn't get enough to eat, but you mustn't be worried on that account. If you would see me I guess you would think I got enough to eat. I keep gaining every day. Once and a while we run some short but very often the worst is our bed, that is rather rough. Sometimes I think I would a good deal rather be in a good feather bed, and have you beside me, than to lay in our houses where we only have a few [stands of] brush stuck up to keep the Jonnies from seeing us. But one thing has been very favorable for us since we came on picket: it's been warm and nice. We couldn't hardly wear our coats it was so warm.

But Nat I hope to be with you in a few months now. If nothing happens the time will soon pass. Now I know how you feel Nat but you mustn't get discouraged. I don't know but what I could come home on a furlough this winter but I don't think I had better come do you? My time is so near out and it would cost 30- or 40- dollars and I think I had better wait till my time is out then I can come for good.

The holidays is drawing near now. You must try and enjoy yourself as well as you can for I don't suppose I can be with you. I wish I could be with you and we could take a good sleigh ride, but I feel in hopes that next holidays I can be with you. We may be in New York by that time. We are a rone and rambling crew.

From your ever true and affectionate husband C. McDowell Goodbye Nancy for this time and don't forget me long.

To Charles from Nancy:

Dearest Husband,   *December the 22 1864*

Levy stayed here last night. We expected to hear of a large battle before this time. The papers stated so but I hope that there won't be any while you are there.

They say that Sherman has relieved fifteen hundred prisoners but they was almost starved to death. Poor men. It is enough to make one crazy to think about it. Some thinks that this war will end in two months but I can't see it so. They think this fall will end it. Anyway, I hope it may so that the poor men can come home again.

It is all most Christmas and New Year. I hope that we will be together next year at this time and then I think I will be satisfied with my lot. But I am not satisfied with it now. But I can get along with it eight month longer, but I am some time afraid that you will reenlist. But I hope that you won't be so foolish. I hear of so many enlisten. I had drather go without half enough to eat than have you enlist again.

I have give up going to school. Axey, she goes to school but I thought I wouldn't go for maybe you wouldn't want me to go. John Muson is married. Rat and Lib Phillips and Dave Courtright and Old Miss Cary, they got John drunk and then got him married to some kind of a thing but he says that he would never live with [her].

From you true and affectionate wife Nancy McDowell

To Charles from Nancy:

Dearest Husband,   December the 26 1864

Christmas is past and gone and I am not sorry, for I am glad when one day passes away and another comes, for then I think you will be home some time or other if your life is sparred, which I hope it may be.

You spoke about getting a furlough and come home. I want you to get it and come home if you possibly can. It seems to me that I would give all that I have got if I could see you once more. If I was sure that you would live to come home I wouldn't say so much about it, but we haint sure of seeing each other again and you are just as able to come home as any of the rest. If you do spend your money, you haint got any children to cry for bread and I think it is your duty to come home if you can.

They are having a dance to South Sodus tonight, at Tom Gulf's house. I wished that you was here to go with me when I see the rest all going. But I am satisfied to stay at home and try and content myself as long as you are in the army.

You said that you did not want me to forget you long. I guess that I won't forget you, no never.

I don't want you to enlist for the sake of getting home for I do not want to spend another three year as I have spent this one nor you either. Any one might better be dead than live so. Don't you think so?

From your true and affectionate wife

To Nancy from Charles:

Camp before Petersburg   Dec the 27-1864
Dearest Wife,
  We are stopping in our old position yet we have pretty good quarters now. We have little log houses. There is five in our house but we can't tell how long we will stay here but I think all winter. I think the war looks a little more favorable now. Sherman and Thomas is giving them fits. I should think they would want to give up. Lee's is the only army that is left that is good for anything and if we could get them from their breastworks we would flay them pretty quick. There is a good many deserting. The rebs are coming in our lines and some of our soldiers are running over there. I saw three hung last Friday for desertion. Some we catched in the valley. We catched 40-or 50- and I believe there is three to be hung every Friday till they all hung. There has been six hung and there is to be three hung this Friday. I think I shall go and see them. I can stand and look on with a pretty stout heart when I think the way they deserted, take the big bounty, and desert and take up arms and fight against us. That is a little too much to stand.
  You say you have been a-visiting. I am glad to hear it. Visit Nat and take all the comfort you can. I wish you a Merry Christmas and a happy New Year with plenty of cider and lots of beer and you may take an extra drink for me for I think we shant have any, for our cellar is rather poor.
  I'll tell you what we had for Christmas. We had for breakfast catfish, soft bread, pork, and tea. For dinner we had pancakes and beef steak and tea. For supper we had tea and hardtack. Wasn't that pretty good for soldiers? I don't know what we will have for New Years but I guess not much better.
  You said sometimes you was afraid I would enlist. You needn't be uneasy about that. If I stay my time out I think I have done my part. Let somebody else try it.
  From you ever true and affectionate husband

  Another soldier, Daniel Chisholm, recorded those weekly hangings:
  "To day the whole division was ordered out to see the execution of three deserters. We moved about a half a mile to the rear of our camp

and formed in hollow square. The men looked clean and nice, their guns glistened in the sun which shines nice, but the air is raw and cold. At half past eleven we heard the brass band strike up the dead march and move slowly from Division Head Quarters. The Gallows was already up and the graves dug and the men could look down in them as they was led up the steps of the Gallows, on they came and passed through a gap that was made through the Square. First came the band then the three poor devils and then a file of twelve men before and twelve behind—They was led up one under each rope. Then the priest (for they were Catholics) went to them and pow wayed a while and then the ropes was tied around the neck and a white cap was then drawn down over the head to the shoulder, arms tied behind them and legs tied together. While this was going on you could hear the boys talking in this way, desert us will you, fight against us will you—Old Phil Sheridan happened to know you did he—a little bit sorry for what you have done ain't you. I will bet the little fellow dies game. I know by the way he stands, that big one says another is such a calf he can hardly stand. Someone cold and teeth chattering. I wish they would hurry and not keep us waiting here all day gaping at them Sons of B_____. Now a fellow stands under with a big-wooden mallet ready to Knock out the stanchion at 12 O'clock, he gets the signal, out goes the prop and down goes three poor fellows about three feet but they stop suddenly and commence to struggle. It is an awful sight, I will stop here.—As the word is attention, right face—forward—file right—march. And off we go, I think no more of it until we get our dinners, as that is the next thing on the programme." (Bill Menge and Gus Shimrak, The Civil War Notebook of Daniel Chisholm, New York: Orion Books, 1989) 54-55

PART IV

1865

Chapter Thirteen
Lee Surrenders, Lincoln Shot

To Nancy from Charles:

[Near Petersburg]   *January the 1-1865*
Dearest Wife

    Old Eighteen and Sixty Five has got around and I ain't much sorry either. But time passes fast with us now. It soon will be spring. Now we have easy times. It is awful muddy now. The most we do is to get our wood and that ain't very hard work. I wouldn't care if it would keep muddy all winter.

    There has been a good [many] soldiers buried around here. You may go any way you are a-mind to and you will see graves throwed up. When we went after wood the other day, we found a man's skull laying a top of the ground. He hadn't hardly any dirt throwed over him. I counted twenty-six ball holes in a tree about a foot through. This was done the time we took the railroad and they charged on us but they got badly whipped.

    Some of our regiment got taken prisoners last night. Co. M and some of the other company went out yesterday morning on picket. Our company didn't happen to go, and about two O'clock this morning, we was waked up by the yelling and shooting of the rebs. They made a charge on them. I haven't heard exactly how many of our regiment there was taken. They say thirty-five or forty-two killed, and five or six wounded. Our boys brought in a few of the rebs. They come on them by surprise.

    There is a good many deserting from the rebs most every night and come over here. I think this war will end this winter. It looks more like it now than it ever did before since I enlisted, but we can't tell this war business is very uncertain. But I find most every one thinks so. I hope so anyway. I would like to have it come to an end this winter.

You would have laughed to have seen us tumble out of bed when the rebs charged on our picket line this morning. We tumbled over one another pretty fast. We was soon in a line. We didn't know but they would try our line of battle but they knowed better than to try that. If they had they would have had a nice time.

You said you would like to have me come home on a furlough. I would like to go home as well as you would like to have me come but I don't know whether there will be any more furloughs given or not. I think it will be a pretty hard thing to get one.

Isae Woodruff started for home the other day. He had a furlough for fifteen days. He has been trying for one ever since his father died and if it hadn't been for his father dying, he couldn't have got one.

You say we can afford it as well as any body. Well I think we could, but if we save the money that it would cost me to come home, we can have so much more to spend. You know we will want to go a- visiting some when I get there.

We might happen to get back to Washington yet this winter. When we get orders to move, we don't stop to tell long stories. We hear Dunbar and them other fellows is coming back to the regiment. I hear that Lee has give Lucy all of his property to keep till we comes back, then I suppose he will take her too. I wonder if he washed his face since he has been home. Robert Trevor is most well.

Old Jef Davis is at home now. I helped carry Jef in when he was wounded. I couldn't help but laugh and felt sorry for him to hear what expressions he made. He said it was too bad. He said there was a reb captain come up to him after he was wounded and commenced turning him over to search him. He asked him what he wanted and he said his money and Jef told him [he] would get it for him. He said he put his hand in his pocket and handed his pocket book and the captain took the money out and throwed the pocket book down and a boy came along and he gave him the pocket book for a drink of water. He would almost cry when he told about that. He said he thought it was too bad after shooting him to take the last cent he had. He said they took twenty-four dollars and ninety-five cents, which he had worked hard for.

And he said there was some more come up to him and said, "You are wounded, are you old fellow?"

And Jef said, "Yes."

"Well," they said, "we will be a long with the ambulances and take you to Richmond you dammed Yankees. We will give you Fishers Hill!"

Now I bet you Jeff's eyes stuck out then. And, he said, in about two hours he seen them going back pell mell as hard as they could run and the Sixth Corps after them. He said then he felt glad. This was about now he laid there on the ground till next day noon before we found him. That is what hurts the men so, laying on the ground so long after they are wounded.

They took lots of money from our boys that day. I could have made a thousand dollars if I had a-went around an got our wounded and killed and searched them, but I wouldn't do such a thing but there is lots of them that does do it and the boys had lots of money then.

There is a good many of our wounded a- coming back to the regiment now. There was two come today that was wounded to Monocacy, besides a good many new recruits. There was one come a few days a go, just like John Tree. You know him. The one we had so much fun with when we was at Fort Foote. The boys had lots of fun with him and night before last we left and we ain't seen him Since. I don't think they will look for him much.

It's a- getting so cold. I don't know but we shall heft to set up tonight and keep a fire. It is a-freezing fast. But we had the good luck to make a haul on a couple of blankets the other night when we was guarding baggage. I find a man has to look out for himself here. If he don't, nobody else will look out for him.

My cousin was over to see us the other day. He is pretty sick of the war.

I think I must write a letter to Canada before long. I haven't wrote to them since you left. Don't you think it is too bad it has been so long since I wrote? I feel most ashamed to write now. I shall heft to apologize pretty well. I must write within a few days. Anyway I have had three or four letter from them this summer. Uncle Hiram has been a- trading farms lately. As soon as my time is out I think I shall go and see them

Sometimes when I get to thinking about my native land and what good times I have had there it makes a feeling come over me that makes me feel sad. Little did I think when I left home that I would be gone for seven years. Oh how I long to see my sister Margaret and all the rest, and if I get out of this alive it won't be long before I can see her. She thought [my likeness] an awful sight. She feels pretty bad about us. She is afraid we will never come home alive but I live in hopes that we will come out all right.

And I must tell you what we had to eat for News Years. We didn't draw no rations yesterday and we hadn't nothing for supper last night, only coffee and nothing for breakfast this morning only we got an order and went and bought some bread. So we had bread, beef and coffee, and drawed rations after breakfast. So we had hardtack, coffee and pork for dinner. ain't that pretty good?

It's getting so cold I must draw my letter to a close hoping soon to get an answer. We expect to go on picket now every day but I hope not till it gets a little warmer. I have just heard that they only captured twenty-three of our men.

From your ever true and affectionate husband C McDowell

To Charles from Nancy:

Dearest Husband,   January the 7 1865

There is a good many to home and you might as well come home as not if you can get a furlough.

I hear that Norman York is dead but one can't tell whether it is so or not. They say that John Howard is dead. He went to war and he was taken prisoner soon after he went to war. Stephen [Wager], he is at Philadelphia yet. I hear that he has applied for his discharge. I think that he is foolish. He can't earn anything after he gets his discharge.

You said that you thought three hundred was a big price for that place. Pa thinks that it is cheep at three hundred. He says it is worth four hundred quick. He says that he would be willing to give that for it if he wanted it. It will make a good little home. I want you to tell just what you would be willing to give and then we will know how much to bid on it. I want you to get a furlough and come home and see the place.

From your ever true and affectionate wife to her dearest husband

It is very lonesome around here. There is nothing going on.

To Nancy from Charles:

Dearest Wife, *January the 8-1865*
     There was a man shot here yesterday for desertion. I went and saw him shot. Nathan Bullock has gone home on a furlough. Was any of his folks sick? They say that he got his furlough on that. If we stay here this winter I think I can get a furlough. If I can I will. We don't know whether they will give furloughs this winter or not. They say they think Old Jef Terry[?] will heft to have his leg taken off yet, so Bill Horn was a-telling me yesterday.
     From your husband C. McDowell

To Nancy from Charles:

(Near Petersburg) *January the 13-1865*
Dearest Wife,
     I am on picket today. It is a very nice warm day. It is just like the spring of the year.
     That Vandercoos, you say, wants to know the directions to where Uncle David lives. He lives close by where my father lives. When he gets where my father lives, he is within a half of a mile of Uncle Dave and Uncle Hiram too. He wants to go to Paris by the cars and then take the stage to Burford and then from there to Norwichville and any body there can tell him where they live.
     I am sorry to hear that Norman York is dead but I hope it ain't so. He was a good fellow. You spoke about selling them coats. You can let your pa have one but you needn't sell any more for the price you say you are offered for them. They cost us at government prices nine dollars apiece. The last one that I sent had been wore about a month, the others I most forgot how they was.
     I think Stephen is foolish to take his discharge. I guess I shall have a chance to come home on a furlough this winter. I spoke to the lieutenant a couple of weeks ago about it. He said he was a- going to try and give all of the boys a furlough that hadn't been home and there isn't only about eight that hasn't been home yet. He says he expects an order every day to let so many go out of the company so I think there is a pretty good chance for me to come. If there is any chance I shall take it.
     From your ever true and affectionate husband C McDowell

To Charles from Nancy:

Dearest Husband, *January the 13 1865*

    I feel very sorry for them men that was captured but was very glad that it was not you. You must be very careful when you go on picket and not be takened.

    I think it is most too bad about not writing to your folks before. If they feel as uneasy about you as I do they are to be [pitied]. You had ought to write to them once a month if you don't do nothing more so as to let them know that you are a living.

    Poor old Jeff [Davis]. Can't bob around as much now with one leg. He hated to have the rebs take his money away from him. He wanted to send it to his old [?] that he used to talk so much about.

    I shouldn't think Nate Bullock would be after another furlough. He has had three now. I should think he would give some one else a chance.

    We are going to have roasted turkey for supper and I wish you was here to help eat it. I will eat a good big piece for you but I would a great deal rather you was here to eat it yourself but it can't be so tonight.

    Dave Brower has bought the place there by the schoolhouse.

    From you every true and affectionate wife Nancy McDowell

To Charles from Nancy:

Dear Husband, *January Sunday the 25 1863*

    I am here alone...all but the cats.

    Mr. Traver's wife is buried today. She died Friday. Poor man, how he will feel when he hears of it. He is the same company that you are in. I wish that I could come out there and stay as long as you hafto stay. That would be just what I should like to be with you, for I don't take any comfort the way that we live now. I guess I had better bring some victuals and then it won't cost so much.

    Mr. Burt's sister poisoned herself to death last week. She took arsenic. Miron Tindall thinks that he will get his discharge but I think that he is mistaken about that. I don't [think] that he will get it any more than you will.

It is as warm as summer. The sleighing is all gone again.

They are having a terrible time about Burt and Old Miss Convers. They say that Burt told his wife about it. When she was to Auburn, Miss Convers went and called for a room and then sent for Wood and he come and stayed as long as he wanted to, and when he went, she sent for Burt. They say that [he?] stayed only one night. Miss Burt says that she wished that she knew before she went to see him. She would not went a-near him. But I don't think that he was so much to blame as she was. She is getting to be awful mean. There won't any body hardly speak to her any more.

From you ever true and affectionate wife Nancy

To Nancy from Charles:

(Near Petersburg)　　　　　　　　　　　　　　　Jan the 30-1865
Dearest Wife,

I am on picket today and I came to camp to fetch out the boys a few hard tack and some coffee. We come on picket now pretty often. We come on about once in every three days. We have had pretty cold weather for a few day back but it is quite warm and nice here today.

I guess I didn't tell you how we got some beef the other day when we was on picket. There was a cow deserted from the rebs and came right by our post. She had a bell on. We catched her and tied her up and milked her. Then we held a court martial over her and sentenced her to death but we thought we would keep her till near night so we could milk her again and after we milked her, we took her out one side and killed her. I took the ax and give her a light blow in the head and she dropped pretty easy. You may know she dropped easy because we had to prop her up to knock her down. But I tell you, the beef came pretty exceptionable and the milk too.

The Milk Ration. Courtesy of Hard Tack and Coffee

    We had milk and coffee that day, lots of it, and we took the two hind quarters to camp and we had boilt beef and it went very well and we got enough of tallow to grease our boots once or twice and I tell you the four quarters was lugged off pretty quick. Well that is enough cow story.
    We have got our house fixed up so it is real comfortable. You said you thought I could come home as well as Nate Bullock. I presume I could if I had spoke for a furlough before he did. He spoke for one when he was in the valley. I didn't think anything about getting one till that time. I wrote to you about it but if Carpenter was here I could have got one most any time, but we have got a new lieutenant. But if I got one the first of March, I think I would rather have it then than to have it now. I don't think we will get pay before then and I could bring it home with me. But I wouldn't be much surprised but what we would have peace within two months from now. That's about all the talk here now. They have stopped newspapers from coming in camp for ten days. I don't know what it is for but I can plainly see that the confederacy is completely gave up. We have some deserters come in every day. They tell the same story.
    Bill Wager hasn't done any duty since we come to Petersburg but he is getting most well now. Sometimes I think to myself that I want go home Nat but what I would like to go as well

as you would like to have me come because the cost might be more than the income, and then Nat I should hate to leave you. Our time is passing along now pretty fast. It won't be long now before it is out and then I shall be glad to think I can go home and stay and won't heft to come back. Don't you think that will be nice? I think so, but I shall come if I get a furlough and I guess I shall. He promised it to me anyway.

How does Marthy Wix[?] and her skinny get along now? Waren was down here. He told some pretty rough stories about some of the women around there. I won't mention it.

I hear that Lib York has applied for some of Norman's pay. She must need some money. Has that man Vandercook gone to Canada yet? I wrote you the directions. If he only wants to send a letter he wants to direct it to Norwichville Canada West and it will go all right. We have got some letters from Canada. I ain't wrote yet but I am a-going to tomorrow if I live and you may bet I will give them a long one to make up lost time.

I must go back on the picket line. Write as often as you can Nat.

From your true and affectionate husband C McDowell

I think a good deal about you nights, Nat, when I am walking my lonely beat in front of the rebs, but I hope the time is not far distant when I shaint heft to do that.

To Charles from Nancy:

February the 12 [18]65

If Warren York told a lot of [stories] about her he had better look to home. I would like to know what it was. I thought maybe he has been telling something about me but I can't see what he could tell. I should think they might let me rest a little. I think they have lied enough about me for this year and the year to come. I haven't seen Warren since I come home.

I don't see but what the women gets along well enough except Miss Cary and Mike Tindall's wife. They are two poor miserable things but that isn't nothing to me. I don't see them very often. If I did I don't think I would take much pains to speak to them. I am a-going to behave myself. Let the rest do just as they like. Isn't nothing to me.

>We are having a protracted meeting held here now but the snow is so deep that there can't many get out. Some places it is up even with the fence. Our old John horse is real lame now. You said thought that you wouldn't come home. I would like to have you come home real well but you can do just as you see fit about it. If you don't hafto go many more battles I should live in hopes of seeing your return. You can tell something about it by March if the war is going to end. In to months if the fighting is all done. I had just lieve have you stay your time all out as not.
>
>They are going to have a meeting to our house but there won't be many here. I wish that you was here. I think you was purty savier [?] with that old cow. I don't think I would like to have you court marshal my cow because I would know what the sentence would be.
>
>Samuel Thompson he waits on Polyan Tindall. The boys go with just any girl that they are a-mind to. They are scarce and there is plenty of girls. Lise Thompson nor Jane Weeks can't get any body to go with them. They are too old to take good.
>
>If you don't get a letter from me in some time you will know what the reason is the snow is so deep that I don't think that the stage could get through and the storm isn't over with yet. It is fairly black in the north. I think that old February is going to see what it can do.
>
>From your ever true and affectionate wife Nancy McDowell

To Nancy from Charles:

(Near Petersburg--Fort Fisher)　　　　　　　　Feb the 18-186[5]
Dearest Wife,

>We have got pretty well settled down again. I don't know how long we will stay here but I hope till the war is over. I don't think that will be long. They are getting pretty well cornered up and they begin to find it out. Ten come in our lines in front of us last night. We are so close together on picket we can talk with one another. They heft to be pretty sharp about getting away for they are watched pretty well by their picket men.
>
>We have got a look[out] built here a hundred and forty feet high. They say they can see to Richmond from the top of it. There is no move can be made around Petersburg but they know it. We

are putting up some big forts here. Eighteen hundred men reports to one fort every morning for work.

From your ever true and affectionate husband C McDowell

To Nancy from Charles:

(Near Petersburg)   Feb the 28-186[5]
Dearest Wife,

I have just come off on picket. Two deserters came in last night a post or two above me. There is lots of them comes in every day and night. They say they all know that that they are whipped but some of them won't give up. One of these men said he had a wife and four children and they was a-suffering for food. Our boys trades with them most every day. We trade them soap and coffee for tobacco and other trinkets that they have. They are awful fraid of Sherman and well they may be for he is just taking them right through the bushes.

We have just mustered for six months pay but they say the Pay master is here to pay us four months pay. We have nice weather here. It is getting pretty warm. It would look odd to see so much snow as you have got up there.

You say you feel afraid to stay alone. I wouldn't do it and if you have got any money by you, you want to be pretty careful. Even Dave Cartright if he had a chance he would break in the house and break in your drawer or any other place if he had a chance. He ain't a bit too good to do it.

Sherman has taken Charleston, Columbia and Wilmington. He is a- going through the southern confederacy like a dose of salts. We cheer when we are on the picket line for Sherman. It rather makes the Jonnies hang down their heads. There is a good many of them disheartened and discouraged and I am glad of it.

From your husband C McDowell to his wife

To Charles from Nancy:

Dearest Husband,   February the 28 1865

We have just got a letter from Stephen [Wager]. He has got his discharge. He says that the wages had come up to twenty dollars a month. I hope it is so for I don't think that you get any too much now. I saw Ike Woodruff to Lyons the other day. I should think that they would have them come back so that the rest of the boys could come home. Mike Tindall is getting a bill from his wife. The trial is to come off tomorrow. Pa is going down to see how it will come out. I heard the other day that Nate Bullock writes to the regiment that his folks is sick but they haint.

I sent you the Lyons paper the other day. It tell about Charleston being taken. They are going to draft here. It makes some of the men look wild. A good many is worried about it but it don't worry me. Let them draft. They can't draft me nor mine. They have drafted in Rochester.

Sam Lape sneaks around as if he had stole a sheep but I don't blame him much.

They had a dance to Bill Fowlers and they got a-fighting and one man got stabbed three times in the heed. They say he bled like a hog. Been Button is the one that stab the other man. They don't think that Jane button will live long. I suppose that you heard about Leas Button being dead. I think [I] wrote to you about her. They have got the story [around] again that Norman York is dead but I hope it isn't so.

Mike Tindall supenad [?] a lot of the men there was with York.   James Davenport, George Davenport, Henry Getchell, Elisher Gatchel, Walter Emery. They think it will go purty hard with them. I don't care what they do with such men. They can't serve them half bad enough. I wouldn't be in Sarah place for anything. She must feel bad but I don't pity her much. She ought to have behaved herself then she would have been just as good as any body.

To Charles and David from brother William:

Norwich [Canada] March 5, 1865
Dear Brothers,

Pa received your letter dated February the 3. We was overjoyed to hear from you once more. We begun to think you had forgotten us entirely but it is better late than never. All we hope and pray for is that you may both live to see home again. You said you wanted to know how Granddad was. You said you would like to have a chat with him--oh but so would I. But we never can do that her on earth. He died the 8th of May 1864 and almost his last word was "My God, my God, shall I never live to see the boys again?" But alas he never did. We missed him much.

We heard from Eb. He is home now. Pa has got so out of practice a writing he can't write atall any more and I have been to work perty hard and I can't write very well. You must not think hard of me for writing so little this time but there haint no news.

So goodbye brothers for a little time. They all send their love to you both hoping you may return home safe.

From your affectionate brother William McDowell

To Charles from Nancy:

Dearest Husband,   *March the 5 [18]65*

That place was sold for three hundred dollars. Old Courtright. I drather they would live there than Miss Cary, for she is [a] little too mean to be on the face of the earth. I will send you twenty cents worth of stamps this time and the next time I will send you more.

Our snow is most all gone. There is lots of water now.

Chub's [?] woman is going to have a little fella. She is purty young I think to be in that way.

Norman York is surely dead. It is awful. They say that Lib [his wife] feels awful bad. I haven't seen her yet but I think I will go over and see her as soon as I can.

Pa isn't doing much now day. His horse is sick so that he can't do much and the snow is thawed so much.

From your ever true and affectionate wife Nancy

Roe, along with Norman York, was also taken prisoner at Monocacy. Remembering his feelings upon hearing he was to be released, he wrote: "In our joy over prospective release we do not forget the poor boys who sorrowed with us, but whom we must leave behind us. Sergeant York of Company D,--how he walked the floor, day after day, exclaiming that he must live to get home to see his wife and baby. But even his will can not keep him up. . (Roe 348)

To Charles from Nancy:

Dearest Husband,   *March the 8 65*

    I think they will have Norman York's funeral next Sunday. Lib [his wife] feels awful bad. I feel sorrow for her. She is to be pitied.

    Aunt Clary Wager is a good deal better and so is Jane Button. Her brother come from New York and brought her some medicine and it helps her real fast, but I don't think she will ever get well. I don't think that the consumption can ever be cured.

    Mike Tindall got a bill from his wife. Now he is lawing them to make them pay damage. I hope they will hafto pay for it purty heavy.

    You can't get but five per cent for money now. I think you might better send your money home for fear they will steal it from you or that you might lose it. If you send it express it. Don't send it by any soldier. Dave sent his by Bill Heck [?]. He may not never get it but maybe he will bring it through all right. I hope he won't lose it. It would be purty hard to soldier it for money and then lose it.

    The snow is all gone. It rains now awful hard and I am glad of it.

    They was a-going to have a party to Mr. Martins. Levi Dunbar had one the other night in his shop. He had his Lucy there. I heard he got drunk and he would hug and [kiss] her right a-fore the whole of them. He had whiskey to sell. [Levi] says that he like Lucy and he can't help it.

    I should think that they would make these boys come back again so that some of the other ones could come home.

    Merneba [?] Runnels is married. She married a dean. He is a cripple. She meant to be on the surer side. They won't take him to war.

    I have been in the woods today. Me and Pa went to gather the sap. He has got a sap bush. We are going to make sugar. I will save you a cake till you come home. I wish that you was here to help make it. Don't you think that would be nice? I think it would. I am going to send you the Lyons paper. They have drafted in Sodus. There is lots of them. They squirm awfully. I can't send you pills in this paper.

It is so bad that we can't get to Lyons but I will buy and send them before long. There has been so much water that the cars could not run. They say that Albany is all afloat. Lyons is all afloat. They can't get to the depot to get the mail.

From your true and affectionate wife Nancy

To Nancy from Charles:

(Near Petersburg)   March the 15-1865
Dearest Wife,

We have had orders to pack up and be ready to move at any minute. We may have a pretty big fight here. I think we will if we have any atol and I think we will have it for they have ordered all of the sutlers to the rear.

I had a letter last night from Canada. They are all well but my grandfather he is dead. He was a pretty old man.

We heard about Norman York being dead. I am sorry it is so. Has Lee Dunbar started back yet? I got the postage stamps came all right. I have used them all up aready. I owed a good many. I am sorry your pa's horse is sick.

Well we don't have much to see to here. All we have to do is to see that we get enough to eat and drink and wear and I guess we will heft to look out for the bullets before long, but I hope not for I don't like them little fellows. We are pretty busy fixing up now.

I have heard that Bill Grandy and his wife is about to part. They say she has cut around with the men pretty smartly.

From your ever true and affectionate husband C McDowell

To Nancy from Charles:

(Near Petersburg)   March the 16-1865
Dearest Wife,

I am on guard today and I have just been to head quarters to express a bundle home. You will get it at the Express office at Lyons.

The army is in quite confusion, packing up and fixing around and the rebs seems to be as busy as we are. I think there will be a big move made some way.

It is pretty warm here today and windy. The dust blows sky high.

From your ever true and affectionate husband C McDowell

To Charles from Nancy:

Dearest Husband,   *March the 25 1865*

I was very glad to hear from you and to hear that you are well but was very sorry to hear that you are about to move. I fear that there is some battle going off but I hope that the Lord will spare your life.

I am very sorry to hear that Magrundy [Granddad] is dead. I made great calculations on seeing him when we went to Canada but we can't never see him. Clinton Hart's wife is dead. They thought that Aunt Clary was dying but she is a little better now.

Stephen Wager just got home today. He has got his discharge. He is awful put up.

It is so muddy that we can't go to Lyons so you see I can't send you any pills. Just as quick as I can go I will send them to you.

We haven't got Dave's money yet and I am afraid that he will never get it. I think it would be a good plan for you to send yours home. If you go into battle the rebs might take you prisoners and then they would take it all away from you. You needn't be afraid if you send it home that I will spend it for I won't spend it any quicker than you will.

From your ever true and affectionate wife Nancy M McDowell

"On the night of April 1st, as soon as it was dark enough to conceal operations from the enemy, the camps became an indescribable scene of activity. Tents are struck; baggage packed; wagons loaded...

"At 4 o'clock a boom of artillery from Fort Fisher is the signal, and the commands, 'Up, men!' 'Forward!' follow quickly. The enemy's picket line is driven in without firing a gun...At points hand-to-hand conflicts ensue; many of the confederates throw down their arms, surrender easily, and seem glad to be sent to the rear of the Union lines...Another four-gun battery was taken, and the Confederates, rallying, re-took and held it for a little time.

"The [New York Ninth] also brought up and put in position the two guns first captured. The retaken fort, after a duel of about one-half hour, in which the Union men worked the rebel guns against them, was recaptured and permanently held. In it was found a corporal with his head shot away, and several cannoneers killed or severely wounded. The whole division swept along the enemy's fortifications to the left as far as Hatcher's Run, capturing many prisoners and twelve pieces of artillery. From Hatcher's Run the troops were hastened back, passed the place where the first attack was made, and formed fronting Petersburgh, and supporting the Ninth Army Corps. Here they bivouacked for the night. Such was the work of Sunday, April 2nd, 1865...

"On the morning of the 3d, the good news was received that Petersburgh was evacuated. The march was then commenced towards Burkeville Junction, and in pursuit of the retreating enemy. The pursuit was continued on the 4th, 5th and 6th. Frequently when there was a halt some good news of the success of the other portions of the army was read, when hats would be flung into the air, and cheers would respond to the welcome tidings. The spirit of the soldier was at flood tide now. On the night of the 5th a position was reached where it was thought the enemy would be likely to give battle, and the time, far into the night, was spent in entrenching. On the morning of the 6th, after a march of about three miles in the direction that the enemy had been concentrated, it was found that they had withdrawn and were moving still further to the left in an attempt to evade an engagement. The pursuit was resumed. At about three P.M. the enemy was overtaken and the battle of Sailor's Creek followed. The Second Brigade to which the Ninth Artillery belonged was in advance of the corps and immediately made a charge upon the enemy, whose policy now was to avoid a fight when he could, but he fought desperately when brought to bay. The charge was made over fields and fences, through woods and swamps, and against a severe fire from the enemy's musketry. Their artillery was also throwing grape and canister. At one time a halt was ordered, that the cavalry might charge. But the cavalry did not charge. The troops were then upon elevated ground, an open field in front sloping down to a bushy ravine, beyond which was another cleared field sloping upwards again where the enemy was re-forming his lines to make a stand. A cavalryman was heard to say, 'It is murder to charge that line—see, they are waiting for us!'

"The infantry charged. The enemy, after making an obstinate resistance, were routed and many prisoners taken...

The troops moved about two and one-half miles from the battle field following the remnant of Lee's retreating army and bivouacked for the night. At 10 P.M. of the 7th of April, they crossed the Appomattox River at Fairville, and encamped for the night. The Pursuit continued until the 9th, when General Lee's army, the pride of the confederacy surrendered." (Clark, 614-616)

To Charles from Nancy:

Dearest Husband,   *April the 9 1965*
 I haven't heard from you in a long time. I feel very worried about you. All the rest gets letters from their folks but I can't get any. Mira got a letter from Dave on Monday. He didn't say anything about you.
 Levy Dunbar and Ike Woodruff they went back in the night. There was men around a- picking them furlough fellows up. The story is around here that they will keep them as much over their time as they had stayed to home. I hope they will for I don't think they done the fair thing.
 Nel Dunbar is drafted. He is around tonight to see who will throw in some money for him to hire him a substitute. I hope that he won't get any throwed in. I think that he is the one that ought to go.
 We hear that Richmond and Petersburg is taken and that they have got Old Lee a prisoner. I hope it is all so. The cannons roars here tonight. I hope it is for some good news for I like to hear good news. I hope the war will soon be over so that the poor men can come home to there loved ones. I think that will be all that I will ask for is to have you with me. Dave Courtright has gone for a substitute. Miss Cary is around crying. She had aught- to be hurted for acting as she does. Abram Wager is drafted and I am glad [of] it. I wish all the old democrats was drafted.
 Mat has got him a new buggy. Aunt Clary is very sick yet. I sat up with her last Sunday night.
 I haven't heard from the Ninth since the battle of Richmond. I long to hear from them so that I can be at rest again. It worries me half to death to think what danger you are in. I hope that I will see the time when I shant have such trouble.
 There was a fox just went by the door. There was a dog after it.
 John Vannatwerp must caught the consumption from his wife. It is too bad.

We have got six hundred and fifty four dollars. I think that is purty good.
From your ever true and affectionate wife Nancy McDowell

On the 11th the march was resumed, and on the 13th the Sixth Corps went into camp at Burkville. (Clark, 616)

April 14, 1865: Lincoln is shot in the head by Booth while attending a play at Ford's Theater in Washington. Booth's accomplice also stabs Secretary of State Seward several times. Seward lives [see Addendum] but Lincoln does not.

To Charles from Nancy:

Dearest Husband,   *April the 20 1865*
Billy Wager is to home now but he did not get home time enough to see his mother. He feels bad.
Don't you think that Lew Williams goes and stays with Miss Cary? She can't get along without a bedfellow. I thought that Lew was more of a man than that. Miss Cary lives in Alton so he has it purty handy. Williams' wife is off some place to her cousins. She has been gone two months so I suppose he couldn't stand any longer. I hope that he will catch the itch. She has got enough to supply the whole...
I hear that Tom York is dead. Do you hear anything about it?
Lib York was over to borrow money of me the other day. She wanted it to get her black clothes with but I did not lend her any. She had aught to have been as saving of her money as I have been, then she would have had some.
I hear that Jonston had surrendered up his whole army to Grant. I hope that he has. They say that Old Jeff is trying to leave the country. He has robbed the banks. He has got sixteen million of specie with him. I hope that they will catch the old scamp. He has done enough to hang him if he had his just due.
Old Booths didn't make much. Do you think that he did? They think that Seward and his sons is out of danger.
From you ever true and affectionate wife Nancy McDowell Goodbye for a while.

Chapter Fourteen
Mustered Out

To Nancy from Charles:

(Near Burkeville Station)   *April the 23-1865*
Dearest Wife,
  We have moved back near Burkville Station about sixty miles from Petersburg. We have laid here near two weeks. We haven't had anything to do since we came here. We have got pretty well rested out.
  We expect to move now most every day. We expect to go to Petersburg or Richmond and from there to Washington or New York. They don't know which yet but we think we soon will get our discharges before long. At least our general tells us so. One thing we know they won't keep such a large army as this any longer than they can help.
  We hear that Johnston has surrendered and Kirby Smith and if that is so there is nothing left of them. One thing is pretty certain-- our fighting is at an end, and I ain't much sorry.
  The army felt very bad when they heard of Lincoln's death. I hope they will catch the band that done it. I think they will get their just due. The dead beats begins to come back to the company pretty fast now. Nate Woodruf, Lee Dunbar, Mon(?) and lots of others.
  You said you hadn't got a letter from me in a good while. I would have written oftener if I could but we was on the go so I hadn't no chance. But before, whenever I got a letter from you, I generally set right down and answered it.
  From your ever true and affectionate husband C McDowell

  That day, "on the 23d a forced march was commenced towards Danville in compliance with orders from Washington to push through as rapidly as possible and assist in the capture of General Joe Johnston's army. The force arrived at Danville on the 27th and halted as General Johnston had surrendered to Sherman on the 26th." (Clark, 616)

To Nancy from brother-in-law William McDowell:

Dear Sister,   *April 29,186[5]*
    We have not heard from the boys since the fall of Richmond. I have wrote to them twice and have not got any answer yet so I thought I would write to you if you would be so kind as to let us know if you have had any word from them since the dreadful fights. We begin to fear something has happened to them. We hope and pray it may not be. We sincerely hope that they may come through safe and sound and have the unspeakable joy of seeing home again.
    We are sorry sorry indeed to hear of the death of Mr. Lincoln. Such a noble and kind man but it may be all for the best. God only knows.
    William McDowell

To Nancy from Charles:

Danville   *May the 3-1865*
Dearest Wife,
    Sorry to hear that you was so much troubled from not hearing from me sooner.
    I am further from home than I ever was before. We started the same morning that I sent you some papers [the] 23 and Bill Wager started the same morning for home. I presume you have seen him before this and he has told you all the news. I am very sorry to hear of his mother's death and sorry that he couldn't have got there before she died. He will feel pretty bad.
    We was rather surprised to hear that we was a-going to Danville instead of going to Richmond or Petersburg. We marched from Burksville to Danville in four days and four hours. The distance of a hundred and ten miles. Here is where John Perkins died and Norman York. Dany Roys and Dave Wey and some others.
    We saw lots of darkies coming here. They are as thick as hasty pudding. They are just like a lot of cattle. Some of these old planters is pretty well off. They owned five hundred Negroes. Some of them we foraged a good deal coming down here. We fetch some of these old farmers right down. But there is some good Union folks here and some that would cut our throats if they could get the chance. I don't know what we was brought here for yet unless to

have Johnston surrender sooner. He has surrendered. Now I think the war is at an end.

We expected to start back this morning but we haven't. I think we will start in a day or two. The first division of this corps started yesterday morning. They took the railroad and I think we will. They have got it a running from here through to Richmond and Petersburg.

The woods looks splendid here. They are in full leaf. We lay right near a piece of woods and I have come out in them to write. I wish you was here to see how beautiful they look. I hope it won't be long before we may examine the same beautiful scene together and I think that time is not far distant now. You must keep up good courage a little while longer. I know how you have felt but I hope you will be no longer in such dread. And I for one are very thankful that I am alive and well. A good many times I felt rather down. It looked pretty dark before me but I have been favored with good luck and I hope [it] will continue till I reach home and then I shall feel happier than ever.

From your ever true and affectionate husband C. McDowell
Goodbye dearest Nancy for a short time

To Charles from Nancy:

Dearest Husband, May the 11 1865
I now sit down to answer your kind and welcome letter that I received last [night]. I was very glad to hear that you was well after such a long march.

I had not heard that Dave Way was dead before. I haven't seen Bill Wager yet. Would like to see him very much. I had a letter from Will the other night. He wanted to know if you and Dave was alive yet. He said that he had written to you twice but had not got any answer. I have written to him that you and Dave was all right and that you would be home before long. I should think that they would discharge you now that your time is so near out. Some think that the Ninth will be discharge now soon but I don't know what to think about it. I hope it may be so but I fear that there is no such good luck for you.

You said that you was in the woods. I would liked to have been there with you and seen the beautiful scene for I love to be in the woods.

They have drummed Miss Cary out of Alton. Lew Williams went the same day that she went. Lew Williams and Miss Cary was caught to bed together and he was a- riding her at a great rate and he paid he[r] off in counterfeit money. They laughed at him and tell him that she said it purty cheep. I hope that he caught the itch off her and then I would think he would get the worth of his money.

You wanted to know what Pa was a doing. It rains all the time so that he can't do much of anything. We have lots of rain for this time of year. It is awful wet.

Do you hear anything from your cousin that was in the army?

Jane Button has gone to New York to see if she can get help. I hope that the poor girl can get help.

Stephen [Wager] is going to set at a grocery over there by Chalbinns. I fear that he will spend all of his money and I don't see how he will get along.

From your ever true affectionate wife Nancy M McDowell

To Charles from Nancy:

Dearest Husband,   May the 16 1865

I am very glad to think that you are coming towards home. I live in hopes that you will get home some day or other. Some of the papers says that the Six Corps is on their way home. I hope it may be so for I long to see you home once more.

There is some kind of beasts near. They whip out all the dogs. They have set on them. They think they are panthers. They catch quite a good many sheep.

They haven't seen anything of Williamns since Miss Cary. Some thinks they have run away together but I don't think he would do that.

Today has been awful warm. It will make everything grow if [it] keeps on so. They are all planting corn here now. I will send you some stamps in this letter. I won't send but a few for maybe you won't stay to use them.

From you own dear wife to her dearest husband.

In May and June the remaining Confederates surrender and the Nation reunites.

"The Civil War was fought in 10,000 places...More than 3 million Americans fought in it, and over 600,000 men, 2 percent of the population, died in it." (Ward, Geoffrey, Burns, Ric, Burns, Ken. The Civil War. New York: Alfred A. Knopf, Inc. 1990,page XIX)

More than half the soldiers, North and South, actually died from disease rather than battle wounds. 50,000 soldiers returned home as amputees.

Charles "remained at Danville until the 16th of May, when they removed by rail to Richmond. On the 24th of May, the Ninth Artillery was received with the corps in Richmond and commenced the march for Washington; arrived after a tiresome march at Ball's cross-roads, four miles from Washington on the 3d of June." (Clark, 616)

To Nancy from Charles:

Camp near Washington *June the 3-1865*
Dearest Wife,
I now take the opportunity to answer your kind and welcome letter which I received the other side of Richmond and we haven't had no chance to send a letter till now.

We had a pretty hard march. We march from Richmond to where we are in camp now. The distance of one hundred and a 20 mls. We lay now within four mls of Washington. We expect to be on our way home now in a few days. Now they are getting the papers ready as fast as they can. The boys is in good spirits. A considerable many was sun struck. It's awful warm.

From your ever true and affectionate husband C McDowell

"The regiment remained with the corps and participated in the grand review in the streets of Washington on the 8th of June. The other regiments of the brigade except the Ninth Artillery were mustered out. The Ninth was transferred to the defenses of Washington. However willing the men had been to remain in these defenses before they had been to the front, to stay there now was irksome and distasteful. They were tired of the fuss and feathers of war-like parades. The regiment garrisoned the forts north of Georgetown. Lieutenant-Colonel Snyder's headquarters were at Fort Reno." (Clark, 616)

Grand Review in the streets of Washington. Courtesy of Library of Congress

To Nancy from Charles:

(Fort Tennallytown)   *June the 20-1865*
Dearest Wife,
    I haven't felt very well for a few days back but I begin to feel pretty well now. I have been looking for a letter from you some time ago but it hasn't come yet.
    We have moved from where we was. We lay now in forts around Tennallytown. We lay in fort about a mile from Georgetown. Our compa[any] we are out of the corps entirely now. We expect to start for home before long. Some think we get started this week but I don't hardly think we will. We had aughta to have been home by this time. Some thinks that Snider is a- trying to keep us as long as he can but I don't hardly think he would be mean enough for that, and even if he did want to, I don't think he could. I don't [think] he has got the power because it's an order from war department to discharge all the men that enlisted in 62 and I don't think his influence would go far there.
    I have been over to see Mrs. Feak. She is well. She told me to send her best love and respects to you. Mr. Feak is discharge. They think they will move back in Wayne County this fall. She says she is coming to make you a visit the first thing she does.

I wish you was here Nat to see what a pretty place it is where I am a writing. It's on a desk on a splendid dancing platform in one of the splendidest ___[?] I ever see.

Did you get one of them 150 dollars bonds as you talked of getting one? There is an order come that any of us can take home our gun and equipment for six dollars. I think I shall fetch mine home. The most of the boys is a-mind to take theirs.

Charles's rifle. Collection of Lee and Lorraine McDowell

There was a man in Co B, I don't know his name, went in the canal a- swimming and he took the cramp or something and went down, and before they got him out he was dead.

From your ever true and affectionate husband C McDowell to his wife Nancy Murial McDowell

To Charles from Nancy:

Dearest Husband,   *June the 23 [1865]*
You will hafto excuse me for not writing to you before for I thought that you was at Elmira.

I have looked for you at home every day so I though[t] I wouldn't write but I am sorry to think I did not write. I guess that you won't write till I do. I haven't had a letter in three weeks. I had a paper that did not satisfy me. It didn't have even tell where you was.

Them things that you sent home we can't tell anything about them. There was not anything that I could claim but the Testament and the housewife [sewing kit]. If there was any more how will we tell them apart? That cloth is splendid. I would like to [have] some of it.

I have planted some potatoes and set about 250 cabbages plants and a nice lot of cucumbers and some corn. I was in hopes that you would be home so as to help me take care of them. I heard today that the Ninth was not coming home till their time was out. I hope that isn't so for I long to see you at home.

They are going to have a great times at Alton the Fourth. I wish that you was here so we could go.

Chub Dunbar's wife had her baby. I[t] was disformed. I[t] had no upper jaw. Samuel Thompson and Tom Sneesbee [?] went to Clyde together and they both got drunk and when they was coming home an old Dutch man and woman was coming along. They wanted them to ride with them and they wouldn't so they almost killed them. The poor old man and woman. They took them both up for acting.

I have been over to Mary Ann and stayed all night. You can [tell] Bill that she is well and is looking for him every day to come home.

I have been picking strawberries and canning them for you to eat when you come home.

Rat Philips is dead. He died the 17 of May at City Point.

I have got me a new hat this summer.

From you ever true and affectionate wife Nancy

To Nancy from Charles:

Dearest Wife,   June the 26-186[5]

I now take the opportunity to answer your kind and welcome letter. It come at last. I thought you would be a- looking for us, but we ain't got started yet. But I feel in hopes now that we will be to home in a few days. They are making out our discharge papers as fast as they can. I am most afraid we shant get home by the Fourth. I hope we can, but if we don't, we will have a good time some other day to make it up.

That box that Lee and me sent wasn't to be opened till we got home. But being it is opened, you had better get what belongs to us. The gun sling is mine and that cutlass, a pair of spurs, and some drawers and some other things I can't tell what but all that ain't marked is mine.

The colonel has just gave them orders to make out the papers just as quick as they could. Me and David was down to Washington today. We don't have nothing to do and I get so tired a- laying in camp I don't hardly know what to do with myself. I should have liked to have been there to help you plant your cabbage plants and potatoes but maybe I will be there to help hoe them.

You never have got them things that we sent when we was to Petersburg did you?

From your true and affectionate husband C McDowell

To Charles from Nancy:

Dearest Husband,   *June the 28 [?] 1865*

I now sit down [to] answer your kind and welcome letter that I received last night. I was very glad to hear from you but was sorry to hear that you was not very well.

I am very glad to hear from Miss Feaks. I would like to see her very much. I think if she moved back here I would go and see her whether she come to see me or not for I think she is a fine old lady.

George Knox lost his wife. She had a baby. The baby is alive. Old Mary Dunbar lives to Lockwoods and they say that she sleeps with John Hen [?] every night. Old John Hen takes purty good don't you think he does? I think that piece about Old Jeff was real cute.

Pa is drawing away his oats. He has got his corn all hoed the first time. There is going to be a circus to Lyons the 30. I wish you was hear for I would like to go

John Howard's funeral was last Sunday. He died in the Salisbury prison. He left two small children.

They say that Mike Tindall is about getting married again to John York's widder. She must want to get married I think, to have him with so many yonones and she has got three.

Is Bill Burt there with you? I heard that he was not. Miss Burt hasn't heard from him in two months.

From you every true and affectionate wife Nancy

Charles did not make it home in time to celebrate the Fourth of July with Nancy, but it wouldn't be long after. "The 8th of July witnessed the farewells to the forts, the march to Washington through Georgetown and the taking of the train for Baltimore, supper at Soldiers' Rest or on rations, and then the train for the North, not exactly palatial, for men slept on the floor or on the tops of the cars. Elmira is gained at 9 P.M. on the 9th. Rest for the night is sought in the barracks, on whose floor sleep is wooed till morn. Then the train, the 10th, to Watkins Glen, and boat to Geneva! Here citizens rally equal to the occasion, and prepare a dinner for us, to which we can not do justice because of being marched down to the train; but we dispose of a part of it, and then ride to Syracuse. Food is had at the hotels, and then we go a mile and half to the camp...There was yet work for some ...

The 20th of July is the day which sees the last assembling and hears the final "Break ranks!" Only a few days less than three years from the time when many of these men enrolled themselves, they are clasping hands, and saying "Good-by," perhaps forever. They have drunken from the same canteen, slept beneath the same poncho, shared toil and danger till the ties that unite them are stronger than those of kindred. (Roe 262-263)

There is great joy in Charles's homecoming:

To Charles from sister Margaret:

Burford [Canada] July the 30, 65
My dear brother,

Pop and mother came here last night and you don't know how my bosom thrilled with delight when I read your letter. I felt overjoyed to think you have arrived home safe, and Charly, you don't know how bad I want to see you. You spoke about coming out this fall and you must be sure and come. The reason I have not wrote was because I always expected to hear some bad news, but now that you are home safe I will endeavor to write oftener...

I never expected Charly that you would ever see home again. But you never will see poor granddad again. I scarcely know what to write but I will make up for it in my next [letter].

So goodbye dear brother till I hear from you again. I remain you ever true and affectionate sister M.I Brooks.

New York 9th Heavy Artillery, Company M. 1865
Couretesy of Library of Congress.

EPILOGUE

Charles and Nancy McDowell

Charles and Nancy bought land and built a home on a hill in Alton, NY. Charles resumed farming. His brother David married Nancy's sister Almira. Nancy's cousin Stephen Wager (the one who lost his arm at Cold Harbor) married, had a child, and because he was too weak for heavy work, became a tin peddler, trading tin for rags. His health was never good after the amputation, and he died on New Years Eve of 1868. A summary of his disability application states: "The impeded circulation, which resulted as it often does, from amputation at the shoulder, gave rise to passive congestion of that side, resulting in "Tubeenular Consumption" of the right lung of which he died."

Charles and Nancy had two children, first a girl, May, and then a boy, thirteen years later. Their son, my great-grandfather Gilbert (called Bert), brought his wife Mary Sisson to live on the farm. Bert farmed, built several summer homes in Sodus Point, and tinkered with inventions in his shop. My favorite was his oily-smelling mechanical bed that rolled back and forth on tracks. The noise and movement lulled him to sleep every night for years after his wife died. When asked why he never applied for patents for his inventions, he replied, "It nobody's business what I do up here!"

Nancy was never fond of Bert's wife Mary, who came from an educated family in Lyons, N.Y. In Nancy's eyes, Mary was a lazy city girl who thought she was better than her in-laws.

Charles died of a heart attack in his seventies in 1913 while visiting their daughter's home in Colorado. Nancy outlived her husband by eighteen years. Suffering from a lingering illness, she spent her final months rocking in her chair and looking out the window. Perhaps she was waiting once again for Charles to come to her.

Nancy in Later Years

One afternoon Nancy fell asleep in her rocker before the window and never woke up.

The town felt that they had lost a celebrity. Her obituary states: "MRS. MCDOWELL IS DEAD - SHOOK HANDS WITH LINCOLN. With the death of Mrs. Nancy Wager McDowell at the home of her son Gilbert McDowell, in Alton Friday, the town of Sodus probably loses the distinction of having a resident who could boast of having shaken hands and talked with the martyred Lincoln. Mrs. McDowell, who was 86 years old, died Friday noon after a lingering illness...Mrs. McDowell was born in the town of Rose...She was married in 1860 to Charles McDowell, a native of Canada, who came to America when a young man. Mr. McDowell was a member of the Ninth New York Heavy Artillery in the Union Army and it was while stationed near Washington that his wife had an opportunity to speak with the President. Mrs. McDowell passed nearly a year in that vicinity and many were the pies she baked for the soldiers stationed at the capital. Typhoid Fever caused her to return to Alton to the home of her parents..." ("The Record," Sodus, Wayne County, N.Y. September 18, 1931)

Nancy is buried beside Charles at the bottom of a slope across the road from their home. Although their final resting place isn't the feather bed that Charles had dreamed about, their headstone is engraved with a Bible verse referring to lovers spending an entire romantic evening together -- "Until the day break and the shadows flee away."

Nancy and Charles's son Bert and his wife Mary had two sons, Gilbert and Russell (my grandfather). Gilbert added many acres of apple orchards to the farm. Gilbert brought his wife Nona to live on the Alton farm with his parents, and she lived there until her death. They had no children. It was Nona who typed a few of Charles's letters and hoped my mother would see their historical significance. My mother, a schoolteacher, thought they were too illegible and poorly written to bother with. She stored them in her attic and they were forgotten.

In Nancy and Charles's home was found a small New Testament bearing Nancy's name (in her handwriting) and the date: August 15, 1863. This was the time she lived with Charles at Fort Foote. Inside the cover of the bible is written the story telling how Nancy carried it during the Civil War. It also mentions how her brother died of Typhoid Fever in Key West, Florida

When my great-aunt Nona McDowell died in February 1995, the house was sold. So ended an era of visiting a home rich in family stories and old photographs.

Charles asked Nancy to save his letters. As a result, we have this account of sacrifice, love, scandal, bravery, and unrelenting worry. The McDowells were an uneducated family, yet their simple words took me, and I hope you too, to another place and time, among a family who believed in doing their part to preserve the Union.

Aerial view of the McDowell Homestead in 1955. The home Charles built is among the taller trees near the center. Nancy and Charles are buried across the street.

ADDENDUM

Secretary of State Seward

"The Man They Couldn't Kill"

by

Guy and Wm. Aurand

April 14, 1865, the night Abraham Lincoln was murdered, marked an assassin's assault upon a member of his cabinet that was so violent and swift that it is incredible that it failed. But fail it did; by the most slender circumstances.

The night was dark and a promise of rain hung in the air. The hour was nearing ten as two horsemen rode towards the brick house on Fifteenth Street in Washington City.

Two hours earlier, John Wilkes Booth had determined to act.

Co-incident with his attack upon President Lincoln at Ford's Theater that evening, Lewis Powell was to kill the Secretary of State, William H. Seward. By such a bold stroke Booth hoped to revive the lost fortunes of his beloved South.

Nine days earlier, on the 5th of April, Seward had gone for this customary carriage drive. With him were his son Frederick, his only daughter Fanny, and a school friend of hers. The afternoon was bright and sunny. As they were headed up Vermont Avenue, for some unaccountable reason the young, spirited team bolted. The Secretary attempted to spring from the carriage in a frantic attempt to halt the careening carriage. In so doing he tumbled brutally to the ground. He was taken to his home to recover.

Doctor Norris, an army doctor, found the Secretary's right shoulder badly dislocated and his jaw broken, in addition to numerous bruises covering the body. Surgeon General Barnes and others of the medical staff held an anxious consultation. To complicate matters, it was found that Seward had sustained a brain concussion.

A telegram was dispatched to Auburn, New York, informing Mrs. Seward of her husband's accident. Although being in ill health, Mrs. Seward left the following day to join her husband. She would never see her home again.

A journey of 34 hours by train brought her to Washington late on Friday night.

On the night of April 14, Good Friday, as Powell and his confederate rode into view of the brick mansion, Seward lay in a restless, painful slumber, his useless right arm hanging from the bed.

Unaware of the approaching assassin, the household at Seward's home was in various stages of retiring. The gaslights were turned low.

Dr. Norris had left around nine o'clock after his examination of the Secretary had shown him to be as comfortably settled for the night as his condition would allow. Major Augustus Seward, the Secretary's eldest son, had retired early in anticipation of being called at eleven o'clock to take his turn watching his father.

With the Secretary, in the dimly lit room, were Fanny and an invalid soldier nurse, George Robinson.

William Bell, a 29 year old black 2nd waiter at the Seward's, answered the insistent ringing of the bell. Powell, a strapping, good looking man with black hair, pushed his way inside, stating that he had medicine for the Secretary from Dr. Verdi.

Bell tried to prevent Powell from going upstairs, but Powell kept moving towards the stairs with such authority that the servant was helpless to stop him. He did, however, caution Powell not to walk so heavily with his boots.

As they reached the landing on the third floor, Frederick barred the way. Powell once more stated that he had to personally deliver the medicine to the Secretary. Frederick was adamant and after a short period of arguing, Powell turned as if to go. Taking a couple of steps down the stairs, he suddenly whirled and pulled a navy Whitney from his overcoat and pointed it at Frederick. The hammer fell and there was a click as the gun misfired. Powell's next step cost him the success of his mission, and his life.

Enraged, Powell sprang at Frederick and clubbed him over the head with the butt of the pistol. Frederick staggered backward into his sister's room with his skull cracked and pieces of bone driven into his brain.

Bell, at the first outburst of violence, fled down the stairs and out into the street yelling, "Murder!" Powell dashed the useless revolver to the floor. The bullet meant for Seward lay unspent in the cylinder.

He drew a Bowie knife and rushed to Seward's room, three doors from the landing. As he burst into the room and lunged toward the bed, Robinson grappled with him. With a swing of his arm Powell sent the nurse reeling across the room. Fanny screamed. Seward roused and took in the struggle.

There was no doubt in the Secretary's mind as to the intruder's intent, but he was powerless to help himself.

Powell threw himself at the prostrate figure and began to slash wildly with his knife. Seward attempted to raise himself and received a gash on the right cheek, the knife nearly severing the flesh from the face. The Secretary fell to the floor between the bed and the wall, and Powell started around the foot of the bed to finish the job.

Robinson once more grabbed Powell. As they struggled, Augustus, roused by his sister's screams, ran into the room.

In the gloom, Augustus assumed that his father had become delirious and had arisen, and that the nurse was attempting to return him to his bed. He grabbed Powell by the chest, and Powell slashed at Augustus, cutting him on the head and inflicted a severe gash on one hand. As Augustus wrestled the assassin through the doorway, Powell mumbled, "I'm mad; I'm mad!"

He sent Augustus reeling against the wall and bounded down the stairs. Augustus staggered to his room and snatched a pistol from his bag and returned, but he was too late.

Powell had stabbed a messenger from the State Department, Mr. Hansell, who had just come out of a hall doorway as Powell reached the lower floor.

Still wielding the knife, he dashed through the door and into the night, mounted, and spurred away.

Bell ran into the house followed by three soldiers from General Augur's headquarters nearby.

Dr. Verdi and Surgeon General Barnes were frantically summoned.

The spattered blood upon the bed clothes, the floor, and even the door knobs; the horribly gashed body of her husband, and the unconscious Frederick, was so great a shock to Mrs. Seward that she never fully recovered from its effects.

The days that followed were anxious ones for the family. The Secretary's condition was rendered critical from the loss of blood and shock from his wounds.

Frederick lay unconscious for 48 hours. Three separate probings were made by the surgeons before they removed all the pieces of splintered bone from his brain. It was two weeks before he was fully conscious, and then he was too prostrate with weakness, his life was feared for. He would spend months in recuperation.

Seward would lapse for hours into a stupor. When Lincoln's funeral procession passed, he was brought to a window and propped up with pillows. The huge black catafalque with its flowing sable plumes went by.

Days passed and the Secretary gradually recovered. By May 21 he was well enough to play his favorite game of whist and read the papers.

But then another cruel blow. Nine weeks after the attack, the Secretary's wife died. In delicate health for years, the accident and assault on her family had taken their toll.

Less than three weeks later, Powell was hanged, along with three other conspirators.

Mrs. Seward's remains were taken to Auburn and placed under the shade of a tree in her beloved garden, where friends and acquaintances paid their last respects. Among the pallbearers to carry her to St. John's Episcopal Church a few short blocks away was Baron De Stoeckl, Russian Minister to the United States, with whom Seward negotiated the purchase of Alaska in later years.

Seward's tragedy was not yet ended. His daughter, already suffering from tuberculosis, died of typhoid fever on October 29, 1866 in Washington. She was buried alongside her mother in Auburn at the Fort Hill Cemetery.

Although Seward traveled around the world and visited Alaska, it was to his home in Auburn that he returned and lived out his last year.

On the morning of the 10th of October, 1872, Seward came down stairs to work in his office. After lunch, he complained that he was having difficulty breathing. He retired to his green couch. Surrounded by his loved ones, his daughter-in-law Janet asked, "Do you have any final words for the family?"

"Love one another," he replied.

Seward died peacefully, surrounded by his family, at four in the afternoon.

"The Military Coming of Age of William Henry Seward, Jr."

by

Peter Wisbey, Executive Director, Seward House.

The experiences of Nancy and Charles McDowell and Janet and William Henry Seward, Jr. are similar. Although a private and a colonel, both Charles and William faced boredom, heat, sickness and combat. Their wives suffered the anguish of worry and loneliness, as well as joining their husbands to experience camp life. For William Henry Seward, Jr., however, the Civil War offered an opportunity for adventure and brought out his leadership skills.

It must have been irresistible for William H. Seward, Jr. not to join the Army at the outbreak of the Civil War. The youngest of the three sons of Secretary of State William Henry Seward and his wife Frances, "Will" always displayed a penchant for adventure. As a teenager, he roamed Auburn, was caught frequenting saloons, and worried his mother by recklessly boating on Owasco Lake with his friends. At seventeen, when Will expressed a desire to seek his fortune in the West, Frances Seward noted to her husband, "although he is still young, I am not sure but it may be best to allow him to make the experiment. He is old for his years and self-reliant. If he continues here two or three years longer I do not see that he is to derive any benefit from it and I never had any faith in his remaining longer." [Letter, Frances Seward to William Henry Seward, July 23-24, 1856, William Seward Papers, Department of Rare Books and Special Collections, University of Rochester.]

Will was not an apt pupil and had little interest in a study, but he did have a business sense. After private tutoring and home-schooling by his mother, he apprenticed with an Auburn hardware merchant and later worked for a merchant in Albany. In 1859, he and friend, Clinton D. MacDougall, manufactured and sold letter press copying books and a year later, the two, with Seward family backing, formed the "William H. Seward & Company Bank."

In June of 1860, William H. Seward married Janet Watson of Auburn. The married couple settled into the Seward House, 33 South Street in Auburn, which they shared with Frances Seward, Will's younger sister Fanny, servants, frequent visitors and numerous pets.

Despite marriage and a successful business, William Seward Jr.'s restlessness was unabated. Other members of his family were contributing to the war effort. His father, the Secretary of State, was a key member of

President Abraham Lincoln's cabinet and responsible for both foreign policy and areas of domestic security. His eldest brother, Augustus, was a West Point graduate and Mexican War veteran. During the Civil War, Gus served as a paymaster for the Union forces. Frederick, nine years older than Will, worked diligently at his father's side in Washington as Assistant Secretary of State. The final straw may have been the enlistment of his friend and business partner, Clinton MacDougall, who joined the Army in 1862 and helped to raise the company of solders that would become the 111th New York Volunteers.

In 1862, Will was asked by Governor Morgan to raise another unit of volunteers from Auburn, Cayuga County and parts of Wayne County. When the 138th New York Volunteer Infantry, later reassigned as the Ninth New York Heavy Artillery, was raised, Seward accepted a Lt. Colonel's commission and became the second-in-command. Janet Seward, pregnant with the couple's first child, recalled her husband's decision:

"Of course we talked about my husband's going, but I was in hope he would not have to do so; but one afternoon . . . he came in with his hand behind him, sat down before me and unwrapped a parcel and gave me a large photograph of himself. I knew instantly that he was going to leave me." [Mrs. Janet W. Seward, "Personal Experiences of the Civil War," Worcester, Mass., 1899, p. 6]

The role of commander seems to have suited William Seward Jr. The men of the Ninth New York settled into fort-building, supervised by Colonel Seward. They built or assisted in the construction of several forts around the perimeter of Washington. The proximity to the capital was convenient for the Seward family. Secretary of State William Seward often brought family, friends, diplomats and even President Lincoln to visit the unit - so much so, that the Ninth acquired the nickname "Seward's Pets."

When finally called into battle during the Rapidan Campaign in Virginia in the spring of 1864, Will Seward and his men found themselves up against General Robert E. Lee and his Confederate veterans. The fighting was intense and unrelenting. Charles McDowell's recollection after the Battle of Cold Harbor on June 3rd, that "Colonel Seward shows himself a man and not a coward" suggests that their 23-year old commanding officer was in the thick of the fray. "In the charge he went right in," Charles wrote to Nancy. "He took one rebel with his sword and knocked him head over heels and he got one leg of his pants tore most off on him. He looked pretty rough."

A month later, the men of the Ninth along with other units under the command of General Lew Wallace, faced the confederates of General Jubal Early across the Monocacy Creek near Frederick, Maryland. Badly outnumbered, the Union forces lost the battle but managed to delay an impending Confederate advance on Washington, DC. During the battle,

Colonel Seward was grazed in the arm by a bullet and his horse was shot from under him. It fell, breaking his ankle. Seward crawled into the woods, found a pack mule, made a bridle for the animal out of his silk handkerchief and rode back to his troops. He recovered from his injuries at home and was promoted to Brigadier General as a result of his service at Monocacy. The remainder of the war, was spent away from the fighting in Martinsville, Virginia, as the Commander of the First Brigade, Third Division, Department of West Virginia.

When the war ended, General Seward resigned his commission and returned to his family in Auburn. He operated the Seward Bank and developed land into affordable housing for the middle class of the burgeoning young city. He was a director of the American Express Company and heavily involved in railroading interests in the state. Seward never sought political office like his father, but was an active member of the Republican Party, the G.A.R. and the Union League.

He took great pleasure in his relations with the veterans of the Ninth New York Artillery. He hosted frequent reunions on the grounds of his Auburn home, now the Seward House museum. Alfred Seelye Roe, the chronicler of the unit, noted in 1899:

> To the survivors of the regiment, the presence of the general at their gatherings is always a pleasure. His words, though not many, are carefully weighed and are ever listened to with approval. . . . The men of the Ninth remember him for what he is and what he was. That . . . our colonel is still meeting with us, and likely to do so for years to come, is a blessing for which all are grateful. Every veteran grasps his hand with cordial greetings."

Like so many other young men in this country's wars, William Henry Seward Jr.'s character was shaped by his military service. Although from one of New York's most prestigious families and not much older than many of his recruits, Seward developed leadership and command skills that won the respect of common soldiers like Charles McDowell.

The William H. Seward Monument, Auburn, N.Y.
Seward Homestead in background.
(Taken from The New York Ninth Heavy Artillery)

For more information regarding the Sewards, contact:

Seward House
A National Historic Landmark
33 South Street
Auburn, New York 13021
(315) 252-1283 (phone)
(315) 253-3351 (fax)

RECIPES

"Boxes from Home"

by

Lisa Saunders

Edited by Jacqueline Saunders

Food--something anyone from any time can appreciate. The folks from home took great care and pride in sending their men tasty things. Of course the soldiers were thrilled to receive them - even if they weren't from a loved one. When Charles's regiment arrived at a fort to replace a departing regiment, Charles writes to Nancy about a box that was left behind: "*I took it on my shoulders and took it down to my company and you had better believe they was glad to see it. I told them that it was sent to me from Wayne County and they all thought it was so and I ain't told them any different and I tell you it went good with us. Bill Burt said that [any] old box looked good that come from Wayne County.*".

Nancy's time at Forte Foote was spent baking pies and selling them to the soldiers. Apparently she was a large supplier of these delicacies despite the effort to enforce protection *"against free trade in pies"* (Roe 51).

I do not have Nancy's recipe for those famous bootleg pies, but her great-granddaughter, my mother, is also known throughout our region for her delicious apple pies. She sells them through the Suffern Women's Club to raise money for scholarship funds. I've asked her to share her apple pie recipe as well as other updated versions of recipes for foods mentioned in the letters, such as apple cobbler, since her great grandfather had such an appreciation for them. Also, Nancy's great-great-great granddaughter, my daughter Jacqueline, likes to bake and she and her friend Amy puttered in the kitchen working from old recipes in order to make the Confederate Johnnycakes or hoecakes.

Apple pie

My mother, like Nancy, makes apple pies in bulk. Nancy and Charles's farm had apple orchards, so when apples came into season, my mother and grandmother put together several pies and stored them in their large chest freezer that stood in their mudroom. Now my mother owns a similar freezer and fills them with apple pies every fall. The apple doesn't fall far from the tree, does it?

Charles wrote that Nancy made seventy pies a day with the help of others doing the peeling. My mother believes she probably put some apple filling into one crust, folded it over, pinching the sides together, making small "finger pies."

<u>Pastry for two crust 9 inch pie</u>:
2 cups flour
1 tsp salt
Generous 2/3 cup shortening (Crisco)
4 - 6 tbsp milk or water

<u>Filling</u>
¾ - 1-cup sugar
Dash of salt
1 tsp cinnamon
¼ tsp nutmeg
6 apples
1 tbsp butter

Pastry - Sift flour with salt into large bowl. Cut in shortening with two knives criss-crossing (I use a pastry blender) until pieces are the size of peas. Add milk one tbsp at a time, stirring gently after each addition. Use just enough liquid to make it possible to gather half of dough together with a well-floured hand. Too much water and/or too much stirring make pastry tough. Shape dough with hands into a large thick round disk. Pat down somewhat with hand on a well floured piece of wax paper. I put the wax paper on a marble slab. Put more flour on top of dough. Roll dough with a marble rolling pin. Roll lightly, but evenly from center to edges. When pastry is the correct size, pick up wax paper and drape wax paper with dough over right hand (if you are right handed). Carefully place on pie tin with dough side down. Gently lift wax paper off dough. If dough sticks in some areas, scrape off with floured knife. Tears don't matter too much because dough is easy to patch.

Filling - Combine sugar, salt and spices. Peel, core and thinly slice apples. Stir in sugar and spices. Place apples in pie tin making a high rounded dome of the mixture. Dot with butter.

After filling is placed on bottom pastry in pie tin, put second rolled out pastry on top. Pinch edges of two crusts together so that it stands up around pie. Bake in 425F degree oven for about an hour. Turn down to 400F after 15 min.

I generally spend a day in the kitchen making several pies. I bake only the pies we will be using within the next couple of days. The rest are put in freezer unbaked.

The kitchen and I are covered with flour.
Mary Ann McDowell Avazian

Apple Dumplings

Crust: See crust recipe for the 2 crust apple pie.

Filling:
6 apples
1 tablespoon butter
½ cup brown sugar
1 ½ teaspoons cinnamon

Syrup:
1 cup brown or white sugar
2 cups water
½ teaspoon cinnamon
4 tablespoons butter

Preheat oven to 500 degrees.
Wash, peel and core apples. Mix butter, sugar and cinnamon. Divide evenly into cavity of 6 apples. Roll pastry and cut into squares large enough to cover apples. Wrap apples individually in the pastry and seal. Boil syrup ingredients for 3 minutes. Arrange apples in shallow pan. Pour syrup over all and place in oven for 5-7 minutes. Reduce heat to 325 degrees and bake approximately 1 ½ hours.
Mary Ann McDowell Avazian

Fried Cakes (donuts)

My mother remembers her mother making fried cakes on their farm in Sodus, N.Y. For an extra treat she coated them with sugar.

5 tablespoons butter
1 cup sugar
2 beaten eggs
4 cups sifted flour
4 teaspoons baking powder
½ teaspoon salt
1 cup milk

Cream together sugar and butter. Stir in beaten eggs. Sift flour, baking powder, and salt; add to sugar mixture alternately with milk. Chill thoroughly.

Roll out 1/3 inch thick on lightly floured surface. Cut with floured donut cutter (the hole is necessary in order for the dough to cook throughout).
Fry a few at a time in deep fat (turn deep electric frying pan to 375 degrees) until brown, turning once. Drain. Makes about 3 dozen.

To sugar donuts: When cool, place a few at a time in a paper bag with confectioners or granulated sugar and shake well.
Mary Ann McDowell Avazian

Sugar Cakes

Submitted by Sharon Lubitow, Educator, Wayne County Historical Society

When Lisa asked me for an authentic Wayne County recipe, I remembered this one. It came to me in the papers of Emma Taft Ennis (1841-1939). I live in Taft House, a c. 1831 home in Lyons, New York, the county seat of Wayne County. A family member gave me Emma's memories and other assorted papers when my husband and I bought the house.

I thought I should try the recipe before passing it on, so I made it when some friends were coming for dinner. I was surprised by the way the cake turned out. A crunchy top formed—perhaps due to the large amount of sugar. The cake is not so much "cake-y" as "fudgey/caramel-y."

When the recipe called for a pinch or a dash, I estimate that ¼ teaspoon will do. If you are not fond of nutmeg, you may reduce or even eliminate it with no adverse effect.

Emma Taft Ennis's Sugar Cake with Apples

2 cups sugar
6 teaspoons butter, softened
3 eggs
2 cups flour
2 teaspoons ground cinnamon
1 teaspoon baking soda
dash salt
dash ground nutmeg
3 cups diced apple (I used Cripsins—Granny Smith would be a good substitute)
½ cup chopped walnuts

Beat sugar, butter and eggs until well blended. Add flour, cinnamon, soda, salt and nutmeg; beat just until blended. Fold in apples and walnuts. Pour into a greased tube pan or 9" x 13" pan. Bake at 350 degrees for 45-55 minutes (I find that 45 minutes is about right for the tube pan and 55 for the 9" x 13") I have made the cake several times since trying it and found that the crunchy top disappears after a day or so. I have served it with vanilla ice cream and with a warm cider reduction (cook cider over low heat until the volume is reduced by half) Enjoy!

Peach Shortcake

To Charles from Almira Wager (Nancy's sister): *"We have lots of peaches now. They lay all over the ground. I wish you was here to take tea with us tonight for we are a-going to have warm biscuits and butter and peaches and sugar and cream. I suppose it is only an aggravation to think of them but if you had stayed to home you might of had lots of them."*

  The above description of peaches, biscuits, sugar and cream, reminds me of my grandmothers peach shortcake:
Peach mixture (you may substitute strawberries)
2 cups chopped ripe peaches
½ cup sugar
Mix peaches and sugar in bowl. Cover and set aside.

Shortcake:
Preheat oven to 450 degrees
2 cups boxed biscuit mix
2 and ½ tablespoons sugar
3 tablespoons melted butter
½ cup milk

Mix ingredients and spread onto greased 8 inch square pan. Bake 15 minutes or until edges are lightly brown.
Cut into squares and cover with peach mixture and whipped cream.
Ida McDowell

Molasses Cookies

To Nancy from Charles: *"I hadn't shaved since we started for the front till today and my mustache got so long I couldn't eat molasses very well and I cut it off and most all the rest of my whiskers. The boys don't hardly know me."*

Although there is no mention of molasses cookies in the book, reading over and over again about Charles's delight in molasses reminded me of the molasses cookies grandma always kept handy in the big chest freezer for my grandfather, Russell McDowell.

McDowell Family Molasses Cookies:

Preheat oven to 375 degrees.
2 and ¾ cup all purpose flour
2 teaspoons baking soda
1 teaspoon salt
1 teaspoon ginger
1 and 1/8 teaspoons cinnamon
¾ cup (6 ounce) evaporated milk
¾ teaspoon vinegar
1 cup shortening
1 cup sugar
1 egg
½ cup molasses

Sift flour with soda, salt and spices. Cream shortening and sugar thoroughly; Add egg and molasses. Add milk and vinegar mixed alternately with dry ingredients. Mix well. Drop from spoon onto greased cookie sheet. Bake 8-10 minutes or until done.

Pancakes

To Nancy from Charles: *"We have lived on pancakes for a few days back and fresh pork and potatoes and cabbage and molasses. One day feast and next a famine. We make pancakes out of wheat flour that we captured. They ain't very light but they taste very well."*

Although my mother doesn't make her pancakes from whole wheat flour captured from a Confederate, she does use wheat germ purchased from a store and they are the best pancakes I've ever tasted!

Pancakes
½ cup pancake mix
½ cup wheat germ
¾ - 1 cup milk
2 eggs
1-2 tbsp oil

Stir with wire whisk until large lumps disappear. Small lumps are OK. While mixture is standing it will thicken. Ladle a spoonful or more onto a lightly greased (I use Canola oil) electric griddle 375F. Turn pancake when it bubbles on top. I serve with real maples syrup.
Mary Ann McDowell Avazian

Seward Family Pound cake

The Seward women probably also sent their husbands boxes from home. The following is an updated pound cake recipe based on one found in the Seward Collection:

Pound cake:
1 pound (2 cups) sugar
1 pound (2 cups) butter
1 pound (4 cups) sifted cake flour (sift before measuring)
10 eggs (Mrs. Seward may have beaten the whites and yolks separately, and then added it to the above ingredients, but I didn't)

Frances or Janet Seward's Cake Recipes, Mid 19th C.
Collection of Seward House, Auburn, NY

Mrs. Seward left no mixing or baking instructions, so I consulted cookbooks and found this the most likely method of preparing:

Preheat oven to 325 degrees. Cream butter and sugar. Thoroughly beat in eggs one at a time until total mixture gets light and bubbly. Slowly fold in flour and spoon into two loaf pans lined with buttered wax paper. Bake 1 to 1 ¾ hours. (I tried making it with bread flour, instead of cake flour, because that was all I had. Don't try that at home!! It came out like a brick. My advice is to go out and buy the cake flour.) Some recipes call for adding 1 teaspoon each of vanilla, almond and lemon extract. The Seward recipe didn't call for any extracts but I think that would be a nice addition.

Johnnycakes (or Hoecakes)

1/2 cup boiling water
3/4 cup ground white cornmeal
1/4 teaspoon salt
1/4 cup milk

Stir together and pour by the spoonful onto greased frying pan over a medium to low heat. Flip when edges are golden brown. Serve with butter and molasses or syrup. Not exactly the best tasting meal, but Charles liked the confederate soldiers' meal better than hardtack. And we prefer good old fashioned pancakes to Johnnycakes any day, but if you're trying to feel authentic, this recipe really does the trick.
Amy Lipari and Jackie Saunders

Lemonade

Charles wrote to Nancy: *"There was a woman gave me a nice straw [hat] in Baltimore and a good dinner and a new kind of a penny to remember her by. We got lots of lemonade and stuff to eat in Washington."*

    I'm not sure what Nancy thought of that woman giving her husband a penny to remember her by in Baltimore, but I'm sure she didn't mind him drinking good old fashioned lemonade in Washington. My mom makes it the way I imagine they did in those days.

Lemonade:
6 Lemons
1 cup sugar
6 cups water (approximately)

Squeeze lemons for the juice. Mix juice, sugar and water in one gallon pitcher. Adjust the amount of water to your taste. Throw in a few of the lemon rinds. Store in the fridge. Serve with ice.
Mary Ann McDowell Avazian

GLOSSARY

Cannonading: "a continued discharge of cannon, esp. during an attack." (The Random House College Dictionary, New York, New York, Random House, 1975)

Copperhead: "A Northerner who sympathized with the South during the American Civil War." (The Random House College Dictionary)

Consumption: "a wasting disease, esp. tuberculosis of the lungs." (The Random House College Dictionary)

Dropsy: "an excessive accumulation of serous fluid in a serous cavity or in the subcutaneous cellular tissue" (The Random House College Dictionary).

Hardtack: "A hard, saltless biscuit, formerly much used aboard ships and for army rations." (The Random House College Dictionary)

Johnnycake, Hoecake: "a cake or bread made of corn meal and water or milk."(The Random House College Dictionary)

Pence: "Brit. A pl. of penny: used when the number of pennies is indicated (usually used in combination): four-pence." (The Random House College Dictionary).

Poll tax: "a capitation tax, sometimes levied as a prerequisite for voting." (The Random House College Dictionary).

Shilling: "A cupronickel coin of the United Kingdom, the 20th part of a pound, equal to 12 pence." (The Random House College Dictionary).

Shin plasters: "a piece of paper money of denomination lower than one dollar" (The Random House College Dictionary) People began hoarding metal coins during the war, so the government issued the paper.

Sixpence: "Brit. A sum of six pennies." (The Random House College Dictionary).

Spider: a cast iron frying pan with feet or legs.

Sutler: Merchant that follows the military and sells supplies to the soldiers.

Tick: "the cloth case of a mattress, pillow, etc., containing hair, feathers, or the like." (The Random House College Dictionary)

Typhoid Fever: An infection, often fatal, febrile disease, characterized by intestinal inflammation and ulceration, caused by the typhoid bacillus." (The Random House College Dictionary)

Yellow fever: "Transmitted by mosquitoes…characterized by jaundice, vomiting, hemorrhages" (The Random House College Dictionary)

BIBLIOGRAPHY

Battles and Leaders of the Civil War, Secaucus, N.J.: Castle, 1983

Billings, John B., Hard Tack and Coffee, Boston, MA: George M. Smith & Co. 1887, republished in Scituate, MA: Digital Scanning

Bowman, John S, ed. The Civil War Almanac. New York: World Almanac Publications, 1983

Catton, Bruce, The Civil War, New York: American Heritage Press, 1960

Clark, Lewis H., The County in the Civil War, New York: Clark, Hulett, Gaylord 1883

Cooling and Owen, Mr. Lincoln's Forts , Shippensburg, PA: White Mane Press, 1988

Dosier, Susan, Civil War Cooking: The Union, Civil War Cooking: The Confederacy, Mankato, Minnesota: Capstone Press, 2000

The Civil War Archive Union Regimental Index New York: Regimental histories from A Compendium of the War of the Rebellion by Frederick H. Dyer.

Bill Menge and Gus Shimrak, The Civil War Notebook of Daniel Chisholm, New York: Orion Books, 1989

The Random House College Dictionary, New York, New York, Random House, 1975

Roe, Alfred Seelye, The Ninth New York Heavy Artillery, Worcester, MA, 1899

Seth Cole, Lyons, N.Y., Wayne County Historical Society, 1984

"Letter Book, Ninth NY Heavy Artillery, Seward House, Auburn, NY."

Ward, Geoffrey, Burns, Ric, Burns, Ken. The Civil War. New York: Alfred A. Knopf, Inc. 1990

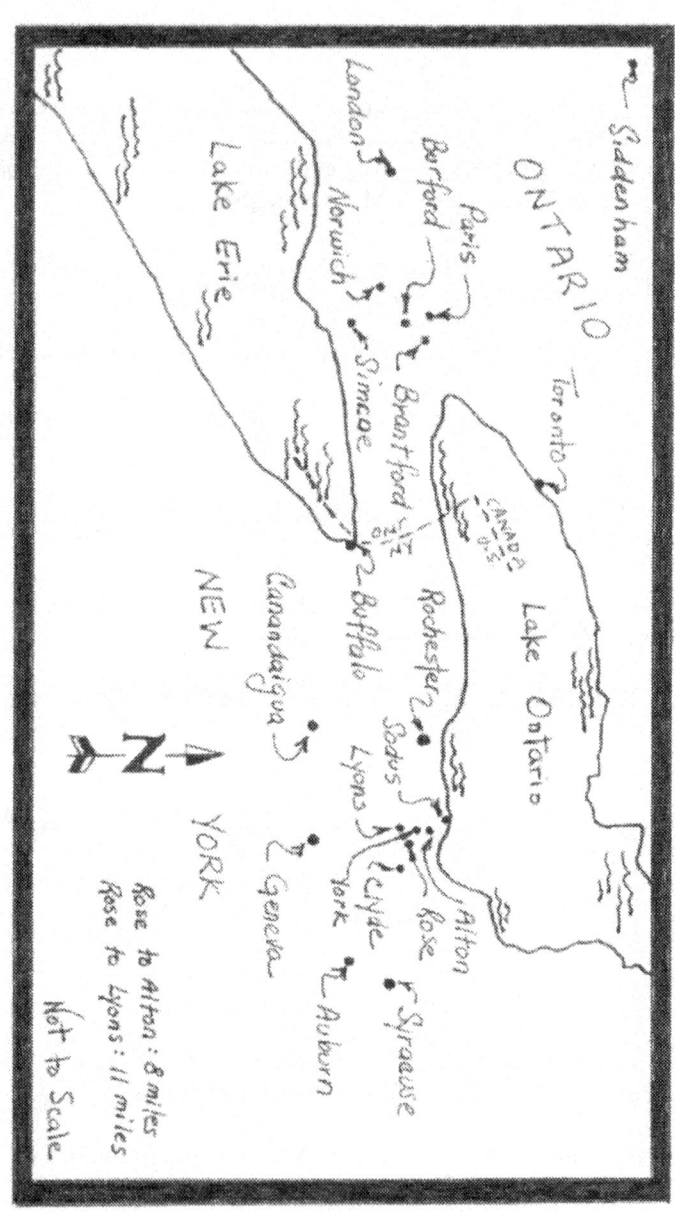

New York/Ontario by Marianne Greiner

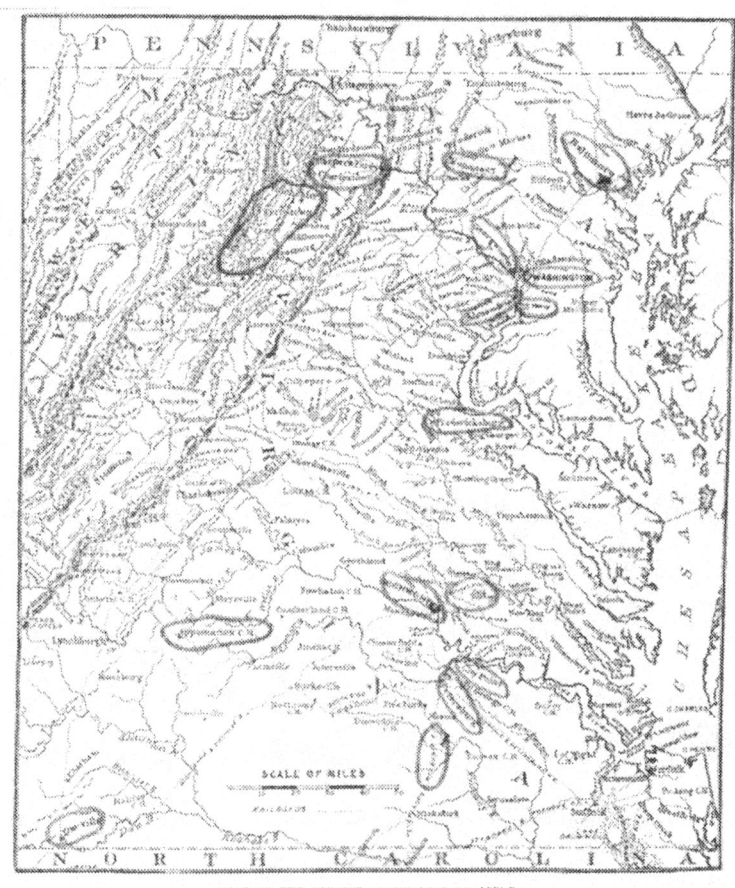

MAP OF THE VIRGINIA CAMPAIGNS OF 1864-5.

The Virginia Campaigns of 1864-65

Taken from <u>The Battles and Leaders of the Civil War</u>

Forts of Washington.
Note circled areas

Taken from The Battles and Leaders of the Civil War

ABOUT THE AUTHOR

Lisa Saunders, a graduate of Cornell University, has also published a children's novel, *Ride A Horse, Not An Elevator* as well as *Riding The Train With Elizabeth*, an inspirational/humorous book about her second daughter born with severe disabilities.

Lisa, her husband Jim, and their two daughters Jacqueline and Elizabeth live in New York's historic Hudson Valley region. Lisa continues to write human interest stories and enjoys speaking to groups and radio audiences. She also researches her other American ancestors and is a member of the Society of Mayflower Descendants, Daughters of the American Revolution and Daughters of the Union Veterans of the Civil War.

If you have any comments about *EVER TRUE* or would like to learn more about Lisa, her work, or upcoming events, visit her website at www.authorlisasaunders.com or write to saundersbooks@aol.com.

INDEX

138th Regiment New York Infantry, 3,5,8,20,28,168
6th Army Corps, xii,78,80,93,115,131,147
90th NY Artillery, xv,xvi,2
9th NY Heavy Artillery, v,12,28,35,49,51,66,77,78,86,92, 115,145, 146,150,152,155,161,168,169
Alton, NY,11,78,82,147,151,155,159-161
Appomattox, xii, 145
Army of the Potomac, ix,xii,18,38,58,72,73,77
Auburn, NY, 3,4,6,9,14,23,37,59,95,135,163,166-170,177,181
Battle of Antietem, 5,6
Battle of Cedar Creek, xii, 115
Battle of Cold Harbor, iii,ix,xii,xvi,63,72,78,79,81,83,94,159,168
Battle of Fisher's Hill, xii, 107,108
Battle of Jerusalem Plank Rd., Weldon RR iii,xii,72,86
Battle of Monocacy, iii,xii,xiii,xvi,36,79,92,94,95,98,99,107,114, 131,141,168,169
Battle of Sailor's Creek, xii, 145
Battle of the Wilderness, 73
Battle of Winchester, xii,107-110,112,115,120
Brooks, Margaret, xiii,22,34,40-42,47,48,132,157
Burnside, Gen., 8,24,29,31,38,69,86
Burt, Bill, v,xiii,8,9,25,80,82,93,97,98,115,121,134,135,156,171
Camp Chase, 5,7
Camp Halleck, 3
Canada, vii,viii,xiii,1,22,34,40,41-43,45,47,48,54,98,100,117,123, 131,137, 140,143,144,157,161
Canfield, Eben, xiii,26,29,30
Cary, Joe and Miss, xiii,70,75,88,92,97,100,101,105,109,119,121-123,126,137,141, 146,147,151
Danville, VA, xii, 36,148,149,152
Desertion (N and S), 127-129,133,136,139
Fort Baker, 72
Fort Barnard, 29
Fort Bunker Hill, 6,7,8
Fort Fisher, VA, xii, 144
Fort Foote, iii,v,xii,50-53,55,56,59,61-70,72,131,161,171
Fort Gaines, 102
Fort Hill Cemetary, 166
Fort Kearny, 8

Fort Mansfield, 13,102
Fort Reno, 35,93,96,97,99,100,152
Fort Simmons, 99,102
Fort Stevens, 98,99
Fort Summer, 102
Fort Thayer, 48
Fredericksburg, 26,27,29,31,35,75,83,87
Grant, Gen.Ulysses S., ix,58,72-74,76,77,81,82,104,108,114,147
Guerrilla warfare, 113
Harpers Ferry, 8,25,96,107,108,112
Hooker, Gen. Joe, 38,48
Lape, Sam, xiii,11,16,26,32,35,68,80,84,87,90,92,117,118,140
Lee, Gen. Robert E.,iii,v,xii,5,18,48,72,73,77,81,82,92,127,129, 130,145,146,148,155,168,
Lincoln, Pres. Abraham, iii,vii,viii,ix,1,3,8,12,18,20,21,24, 25,27,28,31,48,53,58,70,81,95,103,104,106,115,129,147-149,160,161,163,165,168,181
Lyons, NY, 2,3,26,32,37,42,50,57,62,71,74,78,98,121, 123,140,142,143,144,156,160,174,181
McClellan, Gen., 5,9,18,106
McDowell, David , v,x,xi,xiv,xv,1,2,6,10,12,15,17,18,25,30, 33,41,42,45,48,51,57,64,140,156,159
McDowell, John and Henrietta, iii,xiv,1,10,30,45
McDowell, William, iii,xiv,54,140,141,149
Meade, Gen. George, 48,72
Perkins, John, xiii,6,31,35,36,84,90,98,104,114,119,149
Petersburg, VA, iii,xii,82-84,86,89,90,94,99,102,104,114,120,122-124,127,129,133,135,136,138,139,143,145,146,148-150,156
Richmond, xii,24,26,66,72,76,77,80,82,84,89,114,131,138,146,148-150,152
Seward (any family member), iii,v,viii,x,xi,xv,3,7,8,12,20,21,27,28, 32,51,52,53,59,69,77,80,81,94,95,103,147,163-170,177
Sheridan, Gen., iii,107,108,109,113,115,128
Sherman, Gen., 72,79,103,115,125,127,139,148
Typhoid Fever, iii,x,xv,2,15,55,56,161,166
Wager, Almira, v,xi,xv,9,12,16,47,49,50,56,58, 59,62,110,116,159,175
Wager, John, xv,2,88
Wager, Stephen , v,xvi,2,17,23,33,63,64,78,81,82,85,87,92,97, 110,111,119,132,133,139,144,151,159

Washington DC, iii,vii,viii,ix,x,xii,3-9,13,15,21,25,29,31,32,35,37-40,42-44,46,48,49,51-53,58,59,63,66,69,70-72,74,75, 77, 80,85,92-95,97,98,102, 103,107,108,115,120,130,147, 148,152,153,156,157,161,163,166,168,178,184

York, Norman, xvi,46,50,55,56,78,79,95,97,99,114, 123,132,133,137,140-143,147,149

www.ingramcontent.com/pod-product-compliance
Lightning Source LLC
Chambersburg PA
CBHW070657100426
42735CB00039B/2208